The joy of suffering

The joy of suffering

*"God has placed pleasure so close to pain
that you sometimes cry of joy"*

Silvia Márquez de García

Translated by Helda Fryeda Reyes, August 31, 2019.

Library of Congress Control Number: 2019914016
ISBN: Hardcover   978-1-5065-3013-0
                    Softcover   978-1-5065-3012-3
                    eBook   978-1-5065-3011-6

Print information available on the last page.

Rev. date: 17/09/2019

To order additional copies of this book, contact:
Palibrio
1663 Liberty Drive, Suite 200
Bloomington, IN 47403
Toll Free from the U.S.A 877.407.5847
Toll Free from Mexico 01.800.288.2243
Toll Free from Spain 900.866.949
From other International locations +1.812.671.9757
Fax: 01.812.355.1576
orders@palibrio.com
798702

CONTENTS

Dedicatory

I dedicate this book to all the persons who along life collaborated to make me happy. Also to those who supported me in my hardest times of pain and suffering.

To my parents, Ramón and Emilia

Who gave me life and loved me treating to give me the best according to their resources.

To my grandparents, Simon and Juanita

Who made a very important part of my joy in my childhood, from which I keep pleasant memories for their great love and protection.

To my uncle and aunt, Baudelio and Carmen

For their love and kindness, for being so nice to me, immensely benefiting my brothers, supporting them to go on in the United States, so I love and honor them.

To my cousin Consuelo

The only one that remembered us when we were so devastated for our mother's passing away in our childhood, showing her love and concern, sacrificing her Christmas, leaving her family to dedicate to us and preparing a delicious dinner.

To my siblings

Who were the driving force in my existence and reason to overcome in life, very especially to Juanita, Norma, Mary and Nora, who gave me their unconditional support in every moment until today.

To my Uncle Melchor and Aunt Enriqueta

For their love and dedication taking care of my little sister, the youngest one, Aidé Magdalena.

To my daughter Sam

A source of inspiration of God to transform my life and teach me to love.

To my mother-in-law Amparito

Who demonstrated to me her love and support in many areas and she was always there when I needed her the most being more a mother than a mother-in-law.

To my sister in law Lily

For her love and support in the hardest times of our marriage.

To my great friends

Chany and Juanita who offered me their lean to cry on when I was the saddest and most depressed during my youth.

To my children Abraham and Pamela

For their love and support. I cannot reward them for their support and taking care of my daughter Sam the times we have been absent.

To my husband Mario

For loving me when I needed the most, for the sorrows and gladness we have experienced and overcome together, for forgiving mistakes and living a new life full of God's love.

Acknowledgements

First, I thank God for giving me wisdom to write this book and molding me for its purposes.

I thank my friend Laura, who many years ago, listened to my life experiences and encouraged me to write a book.

I thank young lady Ma. José Rivera (Guatemala), who was an instrument of God to give me confirmation that I must have written this book, receiving revelation about how it was going to be helpful for crowds of women.

I also thank young man Oscar Márquez who motivated me to prepare it and edit it besides recording the song with excellence, making me dream big.

I thank my son Abraham who has believed that his mother can make her dreams come true, and I must be an example for him to make his dreams come true, with the Grace and favor of God.

"I honor the youths who are wise, a future of a convulsed world".

1

INTRODUCTION'

"We can rejoice, too when we run into problems and trials, for we know they help us develop endurance. And endurance develops strength of character, and character strengthens our confident hope of salvation. And this hope will not lead to disappointment.

For we know how dearly God loves us, because he has given us the Holy Spirit to fill our hearts with his love".

(Romans 5: 3-5, New Living Translation)

Meaning of joy

The word joy (alegría in Spanish) comes from the Latin *alicer* or *alecris*, which means "alive and lively". It is one of the basic emotions along with

<u>sadness</u> and <u>surprise</u>. It is an inner state, fresh and luminous, generator of general well-being, high levels of energy and powerful disposition.

Joy is an emotion, a constructive action, that may be perceived by any person, being that who he feels it, reveals in his appearance, language, decisions and acts. Sadness is the opposite emotion of joy.

Also it might be defined as a state of the most comfortable mood, one can experience throughout. <u>Sadness </u>is an important factor as without it, one might not feel joy.

Wikipedia dictionary

SADNESS CAUSES SUFFERING

Meaning of the word <u>suffering</u>

1. Feel intensively a physical or moral pain or experience an unpleasant or painful situation, to be afflicted.
2. Bear with patience, a pain or resignation, something that is not pleasant. Bear, endure.
3. Hold or resist a weight, the main walls suffer the forging charge.
4. Be subject to a change, an action or a determined phenomenon, especially if it is negative: the strike has suffered a spectacular increase this month.

Diccionario Manual de Lengua Española Vox ©2007.
Larousse Editorial, S. L.

"Your joy is your sorrow unmasked from the same
stream your laughter comes out. It was many times
filled with your tears. The deeper the sorrows
carve into you, the more joy you can carry in
your heart. They are inseparable. One sits alone
with you to eat, the other is asleep on your bed".
Anonymous

Joy is the result of suffering.

Pain is not an unhelpful experience, as it reveals
myself in a sharper way whom I am.

No one is prepared to suffer. If we could avoid it, we
would do it. We have to be brave people and face it.
Trying to run away will bring more suffering.

Pain and suffering, a universal experience.

No one is free from suffering in diverse ways.

If you lose the joy of living,

You will lose your inner peace.

<u>*INNER PEACE*</u> *IS MORE VALUABLE THAN GOLD,
SILVER AND PRECIOUS STONES OR MATERIAL
THINGS.*

THERE ARE SO POOR PEOPLE, SO POOR THAT
<u>*THE ONLY THING THEY HAVE IS MONEY*</u>...

Money can pay a doctor,

But not health.

It can buy a house,

But not a home.

It can buy sex,

But not love.

THE WORLD HAS BECOME A MATERIAL
WORLD AND HAS NOT COME TO
COMPREHEND THAT MOST VALUABLE
THINGS ARE NOT BOUGHT WITH MONEY:

- *LIFE*
- *BEING A MOTHER*
- *A FAMILY (parents, a husband, children)*
- *FRIENDS*
- *A SMILE*
- *A HUG,*
- *ETC.*

2

HOW SUFFERING AFFECTS

HUMAN BEINGS

Pain is an experience for which every single human being has to go through. We want it or not, there are inevitable pains. There are some pains that once they come, they can be mitigated or eliminated by trying to modify the causes that provoked them. But there are inevitable pains.

Story of a king... who makes a question:

"What will I do to face a serious problem? A wise man drew a vertical line on a board saying? How can you make this line shorter without erasing it?

1. One serious problem can be made smaller _if we manage to get away from it._

2. _If we grow_ as persons we manage _to see the problem smaller"_.

Greek root of the world problem means:

"**THINGS PUT FORWARD**"

Most people in the world are dreamers, they long for success; in the attempt, failures come. They are inevitable and go affecting your heart for good or bad.

Those who mature and learn from failures, lift up again with new strengths and hopes. However, there are persons that act negatively, transforming into frustrated persons, with a hard heart, inferiority feelings, depressions, guilt complex and affective feelings such as hatred, resentments and lack of forgiveness. All those above lead them to psychosomatic sicknesses (they are just in their minds).

The Bible teaches us:

"And we know that God causes everything to work together for the good of those who love God and are called according to his purpose for them".

(Romans 8:28)

All the negative things that happen in our lives should encourage us to mature and become better persons.

A great example we have in this story about how to learn from mistakes in life.

THE STORY OF THE PRODIGE SON

The youngest son asks his father for his share of the estate thinking it would bring satisfaction and happiness, and what happened? It only brought hardship and humiliation, wasting all in pleasure until he ran out of it, and to be able to survive he had to work feeding the pigs and eat the same food the pigs ate. When he finally came to his sense, he said to himself:

"At my father's house even the hired servant have enough food to spare, and here I am dying of hunger! I will go back home and say to him:

Father, forgive me as I have sinned against heaven and you. I am not longer worthy of being called your son, I beg you to hire me as a servant".

All happened to be able to understand
where happiness truly underlies.

UNFORTUNATELY, THERE IS DISEQUILIBRIUM IN LIFE SUCH AS HAUGHTINESS AND PRIDE.

GOD IN HIS IMMENSE WISDOM KNOWS HOW TO TREAT EACH PERSON TO MAKE HIS WRONG WAY RIGHT.

3

FEAR OF SUFFERING

**"He who is afraid of suffering,
already suffers fear"**

Chinese proverb

Frighten, fear, horror

This kind of feeling is related to **anxiety**, the fear of suffering is hard. You are always **preoccupied**.

Preoccupation as its name indicates **is to occupy beforehand of something that has not happened yet, and maybe it will never happen**. Some fears are developed since childhood, adolescence or youth. They are related to traumatic memories and are reflected during adulthood.

"Fear is natural in a prudent person, and being able to defeat it is being brave".

Alonso de Ercilla y Zúñiga

Should you be able to suppose that some people suffer less than others

SURVEY

1. One person voiced that all his life has been so tranquil that has never gone through any pain or intense suffering.
2. Another one answered that he has never been able to be happy, always tragedies come to his life.
3. One said that is a matter of approaches.
4. Other said that it deals with the character, being strong or weak to bear, etc.

There are several fears in people:

Fear of being sick, fear of getting married, fear of not having children, fear of giving birth, fear of something happening to your children, fear of not getting a job, fear of animals, fear of the police, fear of the husband, fear of your parents, fear of your bosses, etc.

One of the most common fears in persons in these last times and most of all because of the insecurity we live is:

FEAR OF DYING

Fear before death is not really fear of being dead, but fear of going through suffering to become dead; most of all, when you are kidnapped, tortured, or before a slow death due to a disease.

Other fear is to know where you go after death

<u>**Jesus felt fear, horror, and anxiety**</u>

When he went up to the Mount of Olives to pray, just thinking of what he was going to go through: betray, hatred, despise, abandonment, humiliation, psychological and physical violence, pain to death on the cross. He felt agony and said to his Father:

"Father, if you are willing, take this cup of suffering from me; yet not my will, but yours be done. Then, an angel from heaven appeared and strengthened him. He prayed with more earnestly, and being in such an anguish that his swept was like drops of blood falling to the ground".

(Luke 22:42-44)

The Gospels tell us that **Jesus started to sweat drops of blood** when he was praying on the Mount of Olives, specifically in the Garden of Gethsemane. It is a medical condition called *hematohidrosis*.

It is not very common, but it can happen when there is a high psychological suffering. A **severe anxiety** provokes an excretion of chemicals that breaks the capillary veins of the sweat glands.

This teaches us that as human beings, fear and frighten is a serious issue, and the best advice is being taken of God's hand to endure the sufferings.

<u>FEAR OF GOD</u>

For an unbeliever, the fear of God is having a judgment from God and eternal death, which is eternal separation from God.

(Luke 12:5, Hebrews 10:31)

For a believer, fear of God is something different. The fear of a believer is worshipping God.

"We are receiving a kingdom that is unshakable; let us be grateful and please God by worshipping him with holy fear and awe".

(Hebrews 12:28)

This worship and awe is exactly what fear of God means for every Christian.

PSALM 112 GIVES CONFIDENCE TO THOSE WHO FEAR

"How joyful are those who fear the Lord
And delight in obeying his commands
Their children be successful everywhere
And an entire generation of godly people will be blessed.
They themselves will be wealthy
And their good deeds will last forever.
Light shines in the darkness for the godly.
Those are generous, compassionate and righteous
Good comes to those who lend money generously
And conduct their business fairly,
Such people will not be overcome by evil.
The righteous will be remembered forever
They do not fear bad news to care for them
They confidently trust the Lord
They are confident and fearless
And they can face their enemies triumphantly
They share freely and give generously to those in need".

DO YOU KNOW THE JOY OF SUFFERING?

JESUS LEAVES TO US A GREAT TEACHING.

What must be done to be able to be a disciple?

If one of you wants to be my follower, you have to turn from your selfish way of leaving, take up your cross and follow me. If you try to hang on to your own life, you will lose it, but if you give your life for my sake and for the Gospel, you will save it.

For, what does a man benefit if he gains the whole world and loses his soul? Or what will a man give in return for his soul?

(Matthew 16:24-26)

"YOUR SOUL IS WORTHIER THAN EVERYTHING THAT THE WORLD AND ITS PLEASURES OFFER"

DOES IT SAY *TAKE ALL YOUR JOY, YOUR MONEY AND BELONGINGS?*

*NO!!! IT MEANS THAT YOU TAKE UP ALL YOUR **EMOTIONAL, FAMILY, PHYSICAL AND ECONOMIC PROBLEMS.***

Call it sickness, indebtedness, lack of work, lack of forgiveness, sorrows, bitterness, hatred, resentments, prides, etc.

THE CROSS IS SYNONYM FOR SUFFERING.

YOUR LIFE IS WORTHIER THAN ALL THE MONEY IN THE WORLD, TRIPS, A HOUSE, A CAR, AND JEWELS...

WORTHIER THAN YOUR HUSBAND

WORTHIER THAN YOUR CHILDREN

WORTHIER THAN YOURSELF

ALL THIS REPRESENTS OTHER GODS AND GOD IS A JEALOUS GOD.

"You must not have other gods, but me. Do not make any idol of any kind for yourself or any image of anything in the heavens or on earth or in the sea. You must now bow down to them and worship them. **For I, the Lord your God, I am the Lord, your God am a jealous God**".

(Exodus 20:3-6)

4

JOY IN THE BIBLE

Joy is one of the main issues in the scriptures. It is found in the Old and New Testament hundred times.

GOD WANTS TO GIVE JOY TO HIS CREATION, GIVE IT SUCCESS AND EXPANSION. HE WANTS THEM FILLED WITH SUCCESS AND PLENITUDE.

The joy translate in men his consciousness of an affectionate realization and the hope that is yet about to come.

Today's world hardly knows this joy which implies a deep unification with God. Most men seek for the joy in which it is not and lose their priorities. They just look for their dreams and pleasures. They accept a quotidian life and with no sense.

Most times the man is shattered in a concrete area of his life such as:

HEALTH

FINANCE

FAMILY

AND MOST OF ALL, THE MOST IMPORTANT:

<u>HIS SPIRITUAL AREA</u>

Not many manage to put together the multiple threads of their existence.

Some characters define what JOY is for them.

Heller Keller: "Joy is an emotion that is reached through loyalty toward a valuable purpose".

Og Mandino: "The true joy lies within you, do not waste time looking for joy outside yourself".

Remember there is not joy in <u>having</u> or <u>getting</u> something, <u>but in giving</u>.

WE SHOULD GIVE HAPPILY:

Give a little from everything we have received.

"You must each decide in your heart how much to give, and do not give reluctantly or under pressure. For God loves a person who gives cheerfully.
(2 Corinthians 9:7)

Joy is important because it makes us become more positive, more creative and can help us reach our goals.

To make others happy we must be happy first. "Love our neighbor <u>as we love ourselves</u>".

Our neighbor is our family. It is not only important to make happy our husband, children, parents, brothers, etc. But we must transmit joy to everyone close to us, and transform our society's lifestyle.

JOY, A MEDICINE AGAINST DISEASES

It is important because it causes positive things that can change our bodies by producing chemicals that help our immune system; therefore...

Joy is in important for our general health conditions.

There are therapies that help our health.

Laughter therapy has helped numbers of people get healed from diseases such as cancer and AIDS.

(Patch Adams film)

SHARE THE GOOD NEWS:

<u>A MESSAGE OF JOY</u>

A message that we must transmit to the world under contradictions, considered as absurd by some people.

The future of mankind shall be building throughout difficulties and apparent contradictions in a world that is not absurd.

- ❖ **<u>BECAUSE GOOD CREATED IT AND LOVES IT</u>**.
- ❖ **OUR JOY** IS EXTRAORDINARILY REALISTIC AND EXPRESSES ITS CERTAINTY: **IN THE VICTORY OF JESUS CHRIST!** AND **IN THE CREATION AS WHOLENESS.**

THE PROBLEM OF PAIN AND SUFFERING IN THOSE WHO SERVE GOD.

Attitudes of those who serve before pain

- ✓ We must wait upon Him
- ✓ We must be patient
- ✓ We have to endure it
- ✓ We must rejoice in Him.

- ✓ Let us not be discouraged
- ✓ Let us not be disheartened.
- ✓ Let us not complain.

WHY DOES GOD PERMIT PAIN?

- ✓ To punish sins
- ✓ To trail us
- ✓ To teach us his will
- ✓ To teach us patience
- ✓ To humiliate us
- ✓ To discipline us with love
- ✓ To impel us to repent
- ✓ To make us depend on his Grace
- ✓ To purify us
- ✓ To manifest His Power
- ✓ To anticipate the good news.

HOW GOD IS RELATED TO PAIN?

- ✓ He keeps control
- ✓ He makes good triumphs over evil
- ✓ He is a shelter for those who believe
- ✓ *He walks with us in the midst of pain*
- ✓ He comforts us.
- ✓ He will end with pain at the coming back of Jesus Christ

HOW MUST BELIEVERS HAVE RELATIONSHIPS WITH THOSE WHO ARE SUFFERING PAIN?

✓ You must pray for them
✓ You must comfort them
✓ You must share their burdens
✓ You must encourage them
✓ You must help them

OCCASIONS FOR HUMAN PAIN

❖ Death of a beloved one
❖ Sickness
❖ Sterility
❖ Physical, psychological and sexual mistreatment
❖ Abandonment
❖ Vices
❖ Children that choose the way of foolishness
❖ Be punished by sin
❖ Suffer for the mistakes of others, etc.

SOME CHARACTERS THAT WENT UNDER SUFFERING IN THE PAST ACCORDING TO THE BIBLE

1. - Stephen was one of the seven deacons, a chosen one.

Everyone liked the idea and chose Stephen (a man full of faith and the Holy Spirit)

Stephen, a man full of God's grace and power, performed signs and amazing miracles among people. One day some men from the synagogue of freed slaves –it was called liked that- started to debate with him. None of them could face his wisdom and the Holy Spirit he would talk.

So, they persuaded some men to tell lies about Stephen. They declared: "We heard him blaspheme Moses". This roused the people, the elders, and the teachers of religious law. Therefore, Stephen was arrested and brought before the Supreme Council.

On that moment, all of the Supreme council stared their eyes at Stephen because his face started to brighten as an angel's.

STEPHEN WAS SAYING THAT HE WAS LOOKING AT GOD'S GLORY AND JESUS SITING ON HIS RIGHT, but they did not listen to him. They covered their ears and began shouting ragged him. Stephen falling down on his knees cried out with a great voice: "LORD, DO NOT CHARGE THEM WITH THEIR SINS". After saying these words, he slept. (Acts 6:5-15)

2. - Job. This story presents the pain of a good man that loses all his wealth, the death of his beloved ones and sickness on his own body without knowing exactly why. God permits Satan to touch him to trail his loyalty.

"There was a man named Job who lived in the Land of Uz. He was blameless, a man of absolute integrity who feared God and stayed away from evil".

(Job 2:3-10)

Being his faith tested, the Lord INCREASED TO TWICE his property he had before, and he had seven sons and three very beautiful daughters.

3. - Daniel was a special gifted-man. He was able "to interpret dreams", see "visions from God". He served though his skills several kings of Babylon. He had a highly-disciplined personal life and "blameless behavior" who served as a model to all those that surrounded him.

He evidenced his "faithfulness to God" by not worshiping other gods. He was incriminated deceivably for worshiping God. He was placed into the den of Lyons and God save his life.

He was placed by the king in privileged places. The example of Daniel proves that we must oppose anything that goes against God's will.

(Daniel 6:1-28)

4. - Paul the Apostle, a testimony of constant joy. He insists on his own life throughout difficulties and obstacles, but just to demonstrate:

That the trail for him has just been a source of joy.

"To prevent me from coming proud of these sublime revelations, I was given a thorn on my body; in other words, a messenger of Satan to torment me. Three times I begged the Lord to take it away, but he told me: «My grace is enough for you as my power works best in my weakness». Therefore, I am glad to boast about my weaknesses, so the power of God can work through me".

"So, I rejoice in my weaknesses, in the insults, hardships, persecutions and difficulties that I suffer for Christ. For when I am weak, I am strong".   (2 Cor. 12:7-10)

Joy is the suffering that can reach martyrdom. It is the sign for excellence of authenticity, we also read:

"You, peoples rejoice along with God's people".
(Rom. 15:10)

All this make us pose this question:

WHY DO BAD THINGS HAPPEN TO GOOD MEN?

As we have been taught that those who do good, things always go well with them; and in the contrary, those who do wrong, always things go badly with them.

GOD ALWAYS ACTS UNEXPECTEDLY, AND AT THE END, WE UNDERSTAND THAT HE ALWAYS ACTS FOR OUR GOOD.

*He gives **success** to righteous men.*

He *is shield* to those who walk in integrity.

*He **guards the paths** of this righteous,*

But the wicked will be removed

From the land, and the treacherous will be uprooted.
(Proverbs. 2:7-8. 22)

WE MUST KNOW THAT GOD WILL CHANGE
ALL OUR SADNESS INTO JOY, AND HE WILL
WIPE AWAY EVERY TEAR DROPPED.

**"He will wipe every tear from their eyes, and
there will be no more death or sorrow or crying
or pain. All these things are gone forever."**
(Revelations 21:4)

I WAS FILLED WITH JOY IN THE LORD MY
GOD! For he dressed me with clothing of salvation,
and draped me with a robe of righteousness. I am
like a bridegroom dressed for his weeding or a bride
with her jewels.   (Isaiah 61:3)

5

PERSONAL LIFE STORY

"JOY AND SUFFERING"

In my life, I have experienced "the Way of the Cross of Jesus". His **stages of suffering and joy of Resurrection**. I think that for those who trust Him and his precepts of life is similar to what he lived. Not like that for those who suffer without knowing Christ"; the feeling is so strong with wishes of not existing. Some in the midst of their weakness reach their purpose by committing suicide. Those as we endure the trail in the bad day, make possible His promises come true,

"If we patiently suffer with him, we shall also reign with him". (2 Timothy 2:12)

MY CHILDHOOD

I was happy to be born in a happy home 60 years ago in a small town in the northern of Tamaulipas, close to the United States border, called Río Bravo to honor the river that many people have crossed to pursue their "American dream", and where many never made it. A totally agricultural area, a piece of God on earth as it does not even appear on a map. I am the second child of nine siblings in my family. My parents' names were Ramón Márquez Dávalos and Emilia Morales Gallegos. I was also joyful to have my paternal grandpa and grandma by my side, Don Simón Márquez Maldonado and Dona Juanita Dávalos Padilla, who used to live next door, first settlers in the settlement. The first ones to have electricity service, and of course, to have a television set. They lived very comfortably. They did not lack anything.

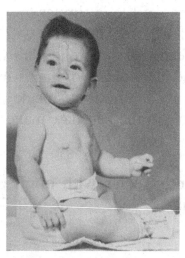

When my second sister was born, she was named after my grandma's name, lovely known as "la nana Juanita". My little sister did not like to stay with her, because she always wanted to comb her hair and she did not want it. She was very unconcerned. When I was born, my resemblance to my grandmother Juanita was very remarkable. Since that moment, she loved me. She almost takes my life. She pampered me very much. She would dress me as her little doll (she was a seam-stress. She used to embroider and knit). She would like to comb my hair. She hugged me and told me short stories. Despite all her chores, she set aside time to play with me. She skipped the rope and sat on the floor and played jacks. She used to take me to the movies and filled me with a lot of presents.

The neighbors would gather together at her home. Every year there was a big party when our uncles came from the United States. All the families got together to welcome them. A small pig was fatten up during the year and we had a big party. Our uncles used to bring presents for all of us without exception. I remember the green van, full of clothes and presents. At night they made fires. Uncle Teodoro played the guitar and my cousin Mary accompanied him singing. My uncles used to make photos modelling without shirts showing their muscles. Other times, there was free movie for all the children in the neighborhood. I remember that all the families that lived in Mexico wanted our cousins to stay over and sleep in our homes, and our privilege was to have our cousin Gloria with us, who was almost my age, but more robust. She was like our mom. She would take a lot of care of us and we were happy. We all slept across on the beds to be all able to fit in the same place.

My mother was a very sad and quiet woman for the marital problems she had with my father, as she discover some infidelities. I remember one day that they argued. My mother was claiming something. Then, she went at my father as a beast and scratched his face. My father defended himself and by taking her hands and taking her down to the floor. Suddenly, my grandmother came in and insulting my mother asked her to leave my father alone. Those memories are very shocking for a 5-year-old girl.

As I resembled my grandmother, I think I reminded my mother her mother-in law. Besides she had a resentment against me. She said that I didn't love her parents because they were very poor, and I was interested in the comforts and presents offered by my paternal grandparents. The truth is that I didn't like to visit my maternal grandparents because I got scared and depressed as they lived one block away from a cemetery. There was no electricity service in their neighborhood. My mother's family was always talking about "ghost and apparitions". They said that before setting there was a lagoon, and at night, "the crying woman" used to appear claiming for her children who got drowned in it, and things like that. They were very poor. They had no place to sit. But that did not make me feel as worried as their stories. That was horror at my young age. But I wasn't a fool girl either. Maybe she was right. I liked to be where there were comforts, I recognize it. Who doesn't want to?

UNPECTED DEATH IN MY FAMILY

FIRST PAIN

When I was about 6 years old, my nana Juanita went to visit her son (my uncle Baudelio) in the United States (Wichita, Ks). I remained sad and counted the days and minutes for her to come back. It became a long wait as she never came back. We were only told that she got seriously sick and passed away. For the first time in my life, I bitterly cried. I think that I almost got insane from grief, as she was my world. My grandpa Simon came back alone, sad and destroyed.

I kept very depressed and crying. I found shelter with my parents. By that time, we were just four little siblings, Juanita, Pablo, Normita, who was a baby and myself. I needed too much comfort. My mother wasn't very affectionate with me. When she lied down to breast-feed the baby, I used to lie down on her back to feel my mother's warmth. I would feel like a little animal looking for protection, so I had to comfort myself without so much attention. My joy was my father when he returned home from work. He was always very caring.

Then, my little siblings arrived and I had to accept that my oldest sister was the spoiled girl. It was painful to find it out. My mom used to say to her best friends and made comments like "Emilia's love is Juanita". Now I was experiencing something that made me suffer as I made her suffer. Well reads the word about the golden rules.

"Do the others whatever you like to do to you. This is the essence of all that is taught in the law by the prophets". (Matthew. 7:12)

SECOND PAIN

Life went on between school and chores at home; most of all, helping wash diapers with so many little kids. My sister Juanita was 17 years old. I was 14 years old, Pablito was a 12 years old, Normita was a 10 years old, Mary was a 8 years old, Norita was a 6 years old, Ramon was a 3 years old, Ricardo was a 2 years old and Aide was a 3 months of age. I was in ninth grade of secondary school. My uncle Bernardino, my mom's youngest brother has just taught me how to drive a car we had; and from one day to another, I started driving it. The next day my mom asked me to take her to see my grandparents, and I think she went to say goodbye, because she started to feel bad, suffered a stomachache. She was given some remedies, but she did not get better, so we went back home. She was out of home making depositions until she just vomited blood. I got really afraid. I called my uncle José, my dad's brother (as my father was working), and he took her to the hospital where she was over three days, bleeding until my father came to look for the oldest ones, who were Juanita and myself to go and say goodbye to our mother who was agonizing.

No, not again! What a pain! I refused to go to see her. I was a coward. I was afraid. I wanted to avoid seeing her die, so I locked into a room and cried all day long until exhaustion. I was very depressed, sad and with no hopes. I pictured things coming to me, "what people will say", and I said to myself: "No one is going to see me crying". "I do not want others feel pity for us". "I am strong" and with a great pride inside me, I did it. Nobody made me go inside the room where her funeral took place. During her burial, I did not want to approach and say goodbye to her. I was criticized by those present. They murmured about my behavior saying "I think she didn't love her" **People are cruel. They don't**

know what you have inside yourself"! So, I became a heard-hearted girl and started to feel very great Resentments.

I didn't care that my parents taught me principles and values about GOD AND HIS GOODNESS. I used to complain by telling him. It is not true that you are good, who leaves many children without a mother? You can't be good! I didn't understand. It was my time as a rebel and I was blinded by grief and suffering.

My home was filled with mourn and my soul too. My character became stronger and my dad used to see that my oldest sister was very naïve and weaker. He began to give me his salary to care of doing the shopping; most of all, the food shopping for our house. I felt very important. My dad started to prepare me, but I didn't understand or I didn't want to. He used to tell me that he was dating a lady, who was from the United States, a widow, and that he might do all the paperwork, and we were going to live there. He used to make jokes at me, and I thought it was just a joke, and the trusted me very much (I was such a fool. He was a handsome 38-year-old man, full of life). My immaturity and my desires that this couldn't happen crumbled before me.

Our pleasure of having him just for us did not last long, as our life was going to go through a big turnaround, and we were not ready for more suffering. We hadn't overcome one thing, and more surprises would come!

Eight months after my mom passed away, he took home the widow lady and with the American documents he talked so much about (which wasn't true), and we met a very young woman, about 21 years old, and besides that she brought with her a 3-year-old daughter, and just like he let us know that she was going to live with us, and he was going to marry her, because he was very young, and couldn't be alone, without a woman. We felt anger and sadness at the same time as he couldn't wait for more time. We still mourned. We hadn't overcome losing our mother, and he was selfish, and he only thought of himself and not of us. We couldn't do anything to avoid it. He already decide it, and there was no coming back.

My sister Juanita couldn't bear the rhythm of living in a second position for our father and with a "**stepmother**". Besides problems arouse such as differences to favor her and her little daughter. We felt **abandoned** also by our father. So, Juanita had a boyfriend for several years, and her getting out was running away with him to escape from this life that we were having.

IMAGINE! ABANDONED BY GOD, BY MY FATHER AND NOW MY SISTER WAS LEAVING ME BEHIND. WHAT A GREAT

SOLITUDE I LIVED. I WANTED TO DIE, DISAPPEAR FROM THIS WORLD. THE ONLY REASON THAT MADE ME NOT HURT MYSELF WAS SEEING MY LITTLE SIBLINGS, SO HELPLESS AND ALONE, I COULDN'T STAND TO SEE THEM SUFFER.

MY STUDIES

My secondary graduation.

I graduated alone, without my family. A neighbor accompanied me. She bought everything for my graduation. I remember her with a lot of fondness. She was a neighbor who supported us much.

God kept me since that time. My sister had had many boyfriends, and I was her companion (her chaperone). If I didn't go with her, I wouldn't let her go out. Sometimes, I blackmailed her. One day a new family came as neighbors to our neighborhood, and I liked one of them. As they were musicians, I was more dazzled, besides that he was handsome, and I said "my sister has boyfriend, why don't I?" He was 19 years old and was a well- experienced, and I was 14. The truth, since he accompanied me and became his little girlfriend, I never saw him again. It was just to say that I have a boyfriend, as he was always busy. He commuted a lot as a band. They had performances, weddings, 15th birthday parties, etc.

What a coincidence! When my mom passed away, he went to visit me after such a long time. He supposedly went to present his condolences. But he had already machinated a plan. He proposed me to run away with him, because they wanted him to marry to a girl, who was pregnant, but the baby wasn't his and I was the one whom he loved. The truth is that his plan did not work out, because I got really afraid and went home running.

AS YOU CAN SEE, EVIL WAS PREYING ME EVERY MOMENT, BUT GOD KEPT ME

I had two choices: **Die** and finish with all the dark world of my life or **overcome** and find a way to go on. I chose the second one, for my siblings. My dad made very little money and there were a lot of shortages at home. We were a family of 12 people, but my 3-year-old baby sister, Aidé Magdalena, was raised by my aunt Enriqueta (my father's oldest sister). She truly deed an excellent job with that baby as at 8 months, she was very healthy and beautiful, and when my dad saw her, he asked her to continue raising her, and that she should always know who her family was and what had happened anyhow.

So, I took heart and enrolled in a Center for Technological Studies in my city thinking of overcoming, and suffering was after me chasing me everywhere. In the afternoon, I used to go to the library to do homework, and my father got very mad at me. He didn't support me and used to say that I was going to become a fool that I just wanted to be in the streets. At school, I had a friend and told her about my sorrows and she told me about hers. She offered me a cigarette in the bathroom by telling me that it was going to help me a lot, so I started smoking when I was 15.

As my father did not believe in me, I got determined to stand out at school with good grades and I gained a half-scholarship in the Company where my dad worked. Even though, he wasn't happy, and he used to overstate that it was just a half-scholarship. I felt much more resentment and anger at him for everything that was going on in our house, but it was not only that, but we experienced something really disagreeable, THE MESS, a dirty house, the tableware remained several days without being done until they got full of worms. My little siblings sometimes made their own food to eat, what they could. I really started to appreciate my mother just until she wasn't with me. That saying is really true. "No one know what he's got, until he has lost it. I was able to find out that I wasn't her favorite, but I missed her! I had imagined her cooking, walking around, picking up everything, and correcting us.

What a great job a mother does!

"SHE IS THE QUEEN AT HOME. THE ENTREPRENEUR OF HER FAMILY. ALL THE

BENEFITS ARE REFLECTED ON HER. WHEN
SHE IS AWARE OF THINGS, NOTHING FAILS
AND HER DIVIDENDS ARE HER CHILDREN"…
WHAT A GREAT TRUTH!

A piece of advice for all the children. Thank God
for your parents, value them and love them. I assure
you for more flaws they have, nobody is going to
love you more than they do. Apparently, they do not
demonstrate it, but they do love us… it doesn't matter
that they love one more than other. We cannot rule their
heart. FORGIVE THEM AND LOVE THEM. Do it
when they are alive, as I have to ask for forgiveness to
a mother who wasn't with me. I think she would have
felt very pleased if I had done it before she died, but
we are never ready to think of death.

"Acceptance of a conflictive and painful situation is the fundamental assumption of each personal progress, with the hope and tranquility to know that after darkness light comes".

LIGHT CAME TO MY LIFE, I LONGED FOR LOVE STORY

A very good friend from secondary school was in love with a boy, and she always would talk very excitedly about him. As time went by, we kept together. Now we were studying a vocational program at the Center for Technological Studies in my city, and she used to tell me that her sweetheart had entered the same school we were. Finally, the occasion came to meet her platonic love, "Enrique", who did not impressed much, but his high stature. He stood out from formation lines, but something started to happen later. When his sweetheart and I passed by his classroom, he stared at me, and I shuddered. I started to blush and feel ashamed about it for my friend, who liked him so much. I kept it inside my heart to not hurt her. I started to fall in love in silence.

Time after my friend and I weren't friends anymore due to gossips and she finally left our school and went to study to another city. Now he was chasing me home, but he would never talk to me. He was really serious. Then I heard that he was with a girl who stalked him, and I lost all my hopes. Finally,

he did not finish school either, and went to study to
the city of Monterrey, N. L. And I remained sadder.
Just coincidences continued to happen. Every time
something was celebrated; that is to say, holidays
or vacation, I would find him in the streets and he
would go after me. Until one day, precisely on May
1 of 1977 when Labor's Day was celebrated in my
country, he managed to talk to me at a party, danced
with me and asked me to be his girlfriend, "If you
wish, give it some thought"- he said. And I answered:
"Yes, I want to be your girlfriend, I already thought
of it for too much time". And that was the beginning
of our love.

MY DIPLOMA

Now I wasn't alone! I had someone who **loved me**. He accompanied me to my graduation. I graduated as an Accounting Technician. Sara, his oldest sister, accompanied us. Memories that are never forgotten. How much I needed to be treated well.

For me, it was as a Cinderella short story, with a prince who already chose me among all his admirers, as he was very popular. My king made me fall in love by letters as he was a little shy, and he hardly spoke, but he would do it quite well by letter, what things he would write me that we indeed **loved each other**.

THE FAVOR OF GOD

The truth is that I wished in my heart to continue studying. I wanted to be a psychologist or a sociologist, but it was not possible due to the economic situation we had at home. I had to work to make my brothers go on. My personal dreams faded away. 1977 was a very important year in my life because a lot of joys came that favorably marked my youth. **The favor of God was with me**. Since that year, I got my degree. My beloved came, and on December 14 of the same year, I was hired to work in a banking institution where I grew for 15 years and I learn to perform myself by serving people. I went through suffering the first three years of work. My first boss was really hard for my inexperience. He used to make me cry.

A work partner was my friend, and I would tell her about my sadness and joy. We lived very close and walked home. However, getting to the corner, I wiped away my tears, so that my siblings could not see me weak. I always had to keep strong for them. On my job, I moved up positions. Six years later I became a counter supervisor. I was the boss of two men. That made me feel important. Then I was an executive, a promotion official. I had my own desk and more authority, so my "ego" raised.

I was financially doing well. My first objective was to fill my refrigerator with food for my little siblings and buy them some clothes as they lacked everything. Then, I got a car for me, remodeled the house and bought some furniture. When my father realized that I had economic power, he started to give me his leadership and allowed me to control almost everything at home. I gave permits and answer for my siblings when there were legal issues or hard situations, etc. I became very independent. I did not ask for permissions anymore. I just informed about my going-outs and coming-backs. I was having haughtiness and more pride than what I already had.

THE MARRIAGE

I was my own God. I became a perfectionist person.
I programmed my life, m children, etc. I decided to
get pregnant after two year of being married, so I
became pregnant of Samantha. I didn't want more
children according to me. I kept working and my
husband's character suddenly started to change. **He
started out with some unhealthy jealousy scenes**.
Wherever we went, if we were in our car, he used
to say "get out, so that you can follow him" and I
replied: Who? I was confused. And at restaurants, he
used to make scenes of jealousy if he sow someone
enter the place. What or who are you waiting for?
I was always crying for so much bitterness that his
insecureness gave me. God knows that it wasn't true.
Jealousy was unhealthy, and made him invent things
that did not exist.

And as Amanda Miguel's song says: "**Now my prince, my king turned into a stone monster, with a stoned-heart. Now he was a king that badly hurt me with no pity, and plunged me in a very deep suffering of resentment and pain**" I was so tired of suffering in life that I asked him divorce, and when he saw I was determined to do it, he asked for forgiveness and asked me to give him another opportunity. Honestly, I did not want to be a divorced woman for **what others might say**, so I accepted him again, but **my heart wounds were already open for so much resentment and low self-esteem**.

MASKS

Even so and fulfilling as a wife, I became pregnant of my second son, Abraham, who was not planned for me and I rejected him, so I had to endure. I thank God as I didn't attempt to do anything against my baby. I kept feeling for my husband nothing but hatred, resentment and lack of forgiveness.

On my job, I was very happy and I was always smiling at everyone. But as soon as I got home, happiness vanished and I was also afraid of knowing that the ogre was waiting for me. I wasn't able to invite my friends as I was ashamed he may be short with them. My choice was not saying a word to him. I sometimes did not talk to him for almost a month. I think I exaggerated and he would get desperate and beg me to talk to him even though I wanted to say bad words to him, that he would stand, but he want me to talk to him. So, I got even like that thinking "that's the way I want to see you, begging me". I not only stopped talking to him, but also ironing his clothes, serving his food or anything else.

When there were social events where we had to go for social commitments such as weddings, we used to put on our happy and enviable marriage mask, and as we got home, we took off our masks, and continued living our bitter reality. The hypocrisy we lived was horrible. Not even my own family found out about our problems. We faked out very well.

SICKNESS

When Abraham turned three months old, sickness came home. My daughter Samantha started to present a generalized convulsion in all her body. I felt like dying to see her, and I didn't know what to do. This scene was shocking, her body contorted and her eyes backward. It is horrible. I ran as a nut. I touched my hair. The baby was crying, and I couldn't hear him. I finally calmed down, and I was able to think of my family's phone numbers because my husband was absent.

We hospitalized her and we were welcome to "epilepsy world". I had already experienced the pain of losing my grandma and my mother and seeing my little siblings suffer more. **The pain of seeing a child suffering is a more intense and painful feeling!**

I would gave my life for my little siblings, but I didn't know this type of pain, and I don't want it for anybody. It was such an immense weigh that when she got sick, I also got sick of sadness and depressed. I felt agonizing. I cried a lot. We saw seven doctors, and they didn't know why she presented convulsions. The resonance test said that everything was normal. Anyway, she was given treatment, and the neuropediatrician said "Neurology is very complex and studies about it haven't ended yet". They shielded behind that, and there wasn't any clinic diagnose.

My husband used to work out of the city. He was absent for long periods, and when he came to see her, he didn't see her have convulsions. By that moment, she had already left the clinic. After two years of having convulsions, it comes the time for him to see one seizure. Honestly, I didn't know whom to help, my daughter or him as he almost got insane of the pain and shock of seeing his little daughter so badly. The truth, I got afraid. That was the trigger for him to get angry and cried out to God why he permitted our little daughter to go through that, and said "why do you torment her and not me, she is innocent". I just asked him to calm down and not blaspheme against God. Since that very moment, we started to recognize our mistakes and ask for forgiveness for all the wrong we had done in our lives. We would offer our lives in return to have our daughter healed. We left behind our marital problems for a while to join us together in our pain and dedicate to search for one doctor after another, so that our daughter get healed.

"The worst nightmares are experienced eyes wide open".

RECONCILIATION

After recognizing our errors throughout we were experiencing, we did have nothing left than turning our eyes upon God as this world could not offer us any solutions, so we received an invitation to Full Gospel Businessmen International's meeting where we received Jesus as our Lord and Savior. And after being some time there, there was a National Convention in our city, and some Prophets from the

United States were invited, and when one of them passed in front of us, stopped and said "you have a lot of lack of forgiveness for each other" and continued saying "God is saying to me that you (Silvia) have a lack of forgiveness for him". He says that he wants to bless you, but if you don't forgive right now and in this place, blessings will keep detained".

Honestly we had problems in all the areas: spiritual, health, family, finance, so my husband and I went to a corner, and he asked me for forgiveness and he said that he forgave me for all I had done to him.

But when he turned at me to take the mask from me, I **lied** to him. And said to him "I don't know why that man said all that", but inside me, I had a great resentment against my husband for so much emotional damage, and most of all for a memory of something he had forced me to do some time ago, consisting in sacking my sister from my house, because he had no privacy. My sister helped me take care of my children. She cleaned the house for me and cooked my food. She was very good and had a lot of economic needs. He said "if you want, we can financially help her, but in her house, so I had to talk with Mary, my sister and told her that my husband wanted her to go. We both cried a lot. I felt a lot of resentment toward him, because I obeyed. But my heart was really hurt for what he made me do against my little sister, whom I loved very much, and there was only gratitude for her.

With that in my mind that I couldn't take away, I could not forgive him. Inside me there was a struggle against with pride, but the words from the Prophet resounded in me: BLESSINGS…blessings for me meant **my daughter's healing**, our financial issues, and family's reconciliation. For me, all the rest wasn't so important, just that my daughter would be healed! For the first time, I bent my pride, **and for the first time, I took off my mask before my husband by telling him everything that had damaged my heart. I told him that I asked for forgiveness for all the resentment and lack of forgiveness I had toward him, and I forgave all what he had said and done to me in the past**.

I don't know what happened, but spiritually something Great moves, so from that very moment, hatred, ill will and resentment were gone. Besides, I could see in my husband all his flaws, now I could see all his virtues. Besides, he had already started trying to conquer me again long time ago, but I didn't allow to happen it. Now I had started to see him handsome and he began to win my heart again. He started by doing such nice things that he wouldn't do anymore. That was something new in him, and he even less dared to say what he felt for me, so he conquered me. I wished to be happy and now I could not deny myself to be happy.

God gave us a new relationship. He made it much firmer than our first love.

It is for that reason that I made this song:

LOVED SUFFERED

Love, how much I have loved you
Since I met you
God started to give me
A great love for you.

Two souls came across
Each one suffering
With very bitter sorrows
From our childhood
Marked our lives
Upside down

Having to be a mother
To all my siblings

While being a girl
A great responsibility

Dreaming about your living
With your precious mother
Living from mistreatment
Marked your character
Your gran indecision.
Finally we came through
Getting married
Not lasting long
Our great happiness

Jealousy overwhelmed you
Which I didn't know about
You hurt my self-esteem.
I couldn't bear
My heartache
For so much humiliation.

My life turned upside down.
And ill will began
I sheltered in "my gods"
Living off appearances
Wearing a lot of masks.

Divorce came to our talks
But everything remained half-done
Sickness came along
Searching for medicine
Without finding an answer

Being us tested
Bending our pride

GOD, YOU ARE SO WISE
YOU NEVER MAKE MISTAKES
YOU TOUCHED US TO OUR BONES
CARVING REALLY DEEP INSIDE.

There was repentance
You came into our lives
You healed our wounds
Gave us a new love.

OUR LIVES YOU RESTORED
NEW CREATURES WE ARE
WE SAW THE MIRACLES
YOUR HAND HAS PERFORMED

HOW WE MIGHT REWARD YOU,
MY FATHER AND BELOVED GOD,
JUST PRAISING YOU
AND GIVING OUR SERVICE TO YOU!

PRAYER

"A DECISION TO FORGIVE"

Lord Jesus!

TODAY I WILLINGLY DECIDE TO FORGIVE ALL THE PERSONS THAT HURT ME FROM THE DAY I WAS BORN TO TODAY.

(IN SILENCE, REFLECT ON THEM, AND SAY THEIR NAMES AND THE WORD, "I FORGIVE YOU").

AND I DELIVER YOU AND DELIVER MYSELF FROM ANY TIES TO WHICH WE WERE BOUNDED. I DECIDE TO LOVE YOU AND BLESS YOU IN THE NAME OF JESUS.

AND I UNTIE THE BLESSINGS FROM YOUR SPIRIT THAT WERE DETAINED FOR MY HARSHNESS.

LORD JESUS, HEAL MY WOUNDS!

NEGLECTFULNESS

Since sickness came home, my attention and care were for Samantha, and my baby Abraham was just breast-fed by me, but my attention was always focused on her, taking care of not letting her got hit when she had a convulsion. Sometimes, I could catch her: other times I picked her up from the ground, her whole body scratched. Her small body got multiples wounds, bruises, etc. Therefore, I neglected my little baby, and when was already 3 years old, my sister Norma made us react about it. We didn't pay attention to our boy, and she told my husband, "you wished so much a little boy, and now that you have him, you don't pay attention to him".

After those words, we reacted, but it was a little late, my boy has turned insecure, restrained, and afraid of everything. Besides that, my mouth would declare very negative things for him. Stress, worries, and anguish plus my marital problems made me a hysteric and loudly person, who said bad words (a curser). As my boy couldn't make it at school, instead of supporting him, I used to insult him by saying words like "You are a fool", "a donkey" "an inept", "you are good for nothing", and effectively, he admitted himself he wasn't capable of anything, and when I would try to touch him, he did not permit it. His sight was hatred itself towards me. I used to say "if you had a gun in your eyes, you would have already killed me". And you know, a spirit of hatred and resentment starts like that in our children, and we forced them towards thoughts of homicide or suicide; plans that later on come true on them.

At home, he has several disagreeable experiences, anybody mistreated him. Children did bullying on him, even girls mocked at him, threw away his lunch, etc. He didn't defend himself. I remember that a boy one day got closer to him and bit his stomach right in front of me, it hurts so much what others do to your children. I could mistreat him, but I wasn't able to bear that others could mistreat him. I just scolded the boy, and asked him "what you did that, he is doing nothing to you". His teacher constantly defended him. She used to say the he was a good boy, but he did not defend himself. The truth, after that, he took refuge in bad companies, joining together with the worst children in the classroom. He made them protect him, and the others didn't get closer to him to mistreat him. He was absent-minded in class. The teacher used to say "he doesn't pay attention, but if a fly enters, he follows it to see where it goes to". Of course, really bad grades.

He not only got fives, which was the failing grade, but answered any test. He even got zero. We had private teachers for him to help him get ahead.

My husband said one day to him, "*Defend yourself*", and my son cried and said, "I can't daddy". "I am afraid of being taken to the principal's office and be punished". His dad answered, "Don't be afraid". "I am your father and now I am here to defend you, because you are not alone, you have a father that is there for you!" It was so nice for me! Now we were in the right way. We had received Jesus in our heart and he has showing to us how to be better parents recognizing such a great hurt we had caused him, especially myself.

We asked our children for forgiveness especially to him for so much psychological mistreatment. I started to hug him and tell him that I loved him because it was something difficult for me. I did hug the girls, but I couldn't hug him since he used to behave badly. Besides that, he had become a liar, and took away other people's belongings, and all that made me turn him down. I had already recognized my mistakes about my son's life, and how I had hurt him making him turn into an insecure, fearful and low self-esteem boy.

I decided to revert all that damage and managed how to help him. I joined the Board of Parents and the school cooperative, so that he could feel confident that his mother was every day aware of him. I saw how he changed. He felt proud of her mother to be in that school position. Later, I did research on help books and found a title "How to make your children's self-esteem rise". I read it and started to apply what I had learned. Now I was declaring positive things, such as "you are great and intelligent", "you have the mind of Christ", "you are going to be a great man", "you will be a great physician-mathematician" (this because mathematics wasn't his thing). He answered, "no, mom. I want to vomit when you talk about numbers". I used to give examples of historical figures, such as Einstein who had not been very intelligent children when they were kids and they had triumphed in life. **I kept doing my job declaring that we loved him, that he was the king of the house, the loved one.**

At high school we made another mistake, enrolling him in a private school, thinking that with personalized classes, he was going to go forward, and it was totally the opposite. He couldn't make it with his classes. He had too much pressure at school, and from us too. One day I was preparing a conference titled **The youths and suicide**. I had a feeling from God that I had to ask my son how he felt about this issue (by starting with your neighbor). I asked him if any feeling of death had come to his mind, and he confessed that he had had a dream, in which he was lying in a coffin saying goodbye to life. I immediately told my husband about that, to ask him to be careful, to not push him about school, his life was worthier than his classes, and if he didn't have capacity to study, he would just work.

So we stopped pushing him. We changed him from school. He failed ninth grade despite our positive attitude, moral and spiritual support. He went to preparatory school. Work about his self-esteem kept going. He was still at preparatory school and I would asked about the major he wanted to study and he answered that he didn't know. God places people to help us. They are like angels that he sends to our lives to help us, so that the preparatory school's principal helped him go ahead. I remembered that he used to tell him, "Abraham, you are a challenge to me", and with extraordinary classes he prepared him very well that and the end he used to get low grades, but the teacher said, "but he by himself figured out all the problems" and applauded him. He left preparatory school by making efforts and without pressures.

We have seen that you can recover our children's love. The Bible says that "Children's heart separate from parents' hearts", and now I was asking God to help me make his heart attach to mine, and I made it with his help.

After supporting him so much, he had a dream of becoming an economist. He is attending now his last year. It is been long, but there is no problem, there is no rush. He will finish his major when God decides it; more years of studying, more experience he will gain. The biggest miracle is that his major is **"Business Calculus"**, thousands of formulas and numbers, and with God's help, he has believed that he is a winner. **He is a successful young man inside his mind and heart**, and now we love each other, and I show so much affection for him, and he accepts it as a baby despite he is 30 years old and is 1.84 m (7 feet) and he is still "my boy", and lets me pamper him.

He is working in American successful company right now he is in charge of important Finances department and leader of 30 people In this year he became worker of the year for the Glory of God.

"Now all glory to God, who is able, through his mighty power at work within us, to accomplish infinitely more than we might imagine or ask"

(Ephesians 3:20)

IT IS NEVER LATE TO RECOVER OUR CHILDREN'S LOVE AND RAISE THEIR SELF-ESTEEM! WHILE THEY ARE IN THIS WORLD, THERE IS STILL TIME LEFT.

Song to my son:

"THE INVISIBLE"

Oh! How I do repent
From the hurt I made you
For not knowing how to be a mother

To a so desired son
I refuge my sadness
Caused by pain
Of seeing the disease
So severe in your sister.
I made a serious mistake
Making you invisible
Not paying attention to you
Hurting by word of mouth
Your tender heart.

What a wonderful God we have
That gives opportunities
To be a better person
Starting over again
With a new life
Full of happiness

I thank my Father
For giving me forgiveness
And to you, my son
Let me show you
That I've been transformed
By showing my love
Giving to you my attention
One day I denied to you
Raising your self-esteem
Changing my words
For positive things,
Blot out our past
Impossible I know it is

It just remains to give you
Something even bigger
GOD AS YOUR FATHER
WHO CAN NEVER LET YOU DOWN

Plans he has in your life
For good, not for evil
To be able to give you
A bright future
Full of welfare
IF YOU HOLD HIS HAND
Nothing is going to happen to you
Life is hard,
But if you keep faithful
Following his path
You will always prosper
As a planted tree
Along a riverbank
Your leaves shall not wither
You will be very strong.

I GIVE HONOR TO GOD
FOR MY HAPPY CHILDREN

DISMISSALS

As I mentioned before, I was my own god. I
wished to have trophies: a job, a husband and
just one child. Children hindered me as my goal
was climbing positions on my job. I was close to
be given a management position. I came pretty

close to build my residence. Besides, another pregnancy would made me loss my body shape. My uniforms were not going to fit me. I just thought of superfluous things, just vanity. I just wanted a daughter and now I am having my third baby. It can be happening. I couldn't forgive myself, and I bitterly cried regretting. But as time went by, God showed me:

"My thoughts are not like my thoughts, and my ways are far beyond anything you could imagine. For just as the heavens are higher than the earth, so my ways are higher than your ways"   (Isaiah 55:8-9)

Precisely when my third daughter is born, there were many changes in our lives, which weren't not very favorable.

The first: Three months after my daughter was born, enjoying my maternity leave, I was noticed from work that I had to go to Human Resources for my severance pay, which was caused by a situation in the bank for which I was made responsible. First depression.

The second: Post-partum depression.

The third: Moving to another city. My husband was transferred on his job to Jalisco. We went to live with him to a place we didn't know.

The fourth. My husband did not stay in Jalisco. He was transferred to Puerto Vallarta 5 days later, about 5 hours away from us. I was alone again to go ahead with my little children, but in a city that I didn't know.

I kept crying with a double depression for all the changes. It was a very hard time. I felt fat (I gained 20 kg during my pregnancy). Upon this, I would get clothes to fill my emptiness and then I was the same. Nothing could fill me, I continued feeling sad. I started drinking. First, I bought a prepared drink. Then, I would buy a bottle of tequila, and everything to prepare for me a drink that I liked "Vampiros". I was sometimes with my children all drunk from the abuse.

Behind my house in Jalisco there was a bullring. Night fell and I locked in my room with my children. And I suddenly heard a strong noise at the back of the house in the yard and then someone knocked the back door. I got really scared and I thought someone was going to get in the house. I had no phone and my room faced the street. There was a balcony and I got out yelling at people to call the police, that someone was in the house yard. Moments later the police came well-armed and told me, "open the door, lady". I was really afraid to come down to open. I finally took heart and opened. They did not find anyone, but just traces of blood on the walls. They went out and three houses away, they saw someone coming down from the roof, and it was the person that was in my yard.

I got so scared that I went to one of my husband's work partner's house, who lived in that city to talk to him and tell him what happened. He and his wife calmed me down. They did not want to call my husband to not scare him, they investigated who the man was that wanted to enter my house, and told him that he was drunk in the bullring and fell asleep. Now he was looking for a place to get out and crossed to my house, that he wasn't a wrongdoer and to be calm. He gave me a radio to keep in contact with him if something happened. After this incident, I couldn't be in peace in that place. But I stopped drinking.

Next year my sponsor is also discharged from work and with his severance payment and mine, he planted some farming land, which did not produced anything. We lived some time there. Due to his worries, my husband felt bad, his blood pressure came down. Something wanted to happen, but I said to him, "Do not get sick, do not die and leave with so many problems". Cheer up, my love!

We came back home failed, with marital problems, sickness in our family, guilt feelings for mistakes made and child neglect, without a job and really serious financial problems.

It is very sad to get to your mother in law's house as a freeloader, because our house was rented, there were five months left for the lease expiration. Our debts came over us, the house pay, due credit cards, lawyers attempting to seize our properties, we, selling off all the valuable things to get ahead.

INVITATION TO FGBMFI

After several months unemployed, my husband got a job to support us a little, and realizing that he couldn't pay with that salary all his payments of arrears, he decided to set up an office with a seed grant; therefore, he looks for an accountant to keep the business records, and we recognized that he was a friend, and his housewife was a former co-worker. The accountant served as President for the Full Gospel Businessmen Fellowship International.

After insisting three times, we went. We were not easy to convince. There was something we didn't like about this organization most of all, the word "full gospel". We felt that it was something like a church, and they wanted us to change our religion. Sometimes, you act just for commitments. The most wonderful thing is that after our first time we went, we felt something special.

The speaker that night shared his experience, very shocking for us as we listened that his son was playing with a gas boat and being near to the boiler, he had caught fire. His mother got out to try to put out the fire, and now they became two balls of fire. The speaker got out, and not knowing whom to put out fire, he went after his son, and the three burnt with third grade burns. At the hospital, his wife was in a room, the boy in another one and while he was fighting between life and death, his wife dies, and he cannot go to her funeral due to his health conditions. She is buried by their children. Miraculously, his 3 year-old child survives ending with a disfigured face. But they leave that place, and that little boy had a purpose because since that age he started to talk about God's marvelous things in his life.

I got so impressed because I had a special daughter, whom we did not accept. My husband, my children and I felt ashamed that she behaved differently. After that experience, I realized that my daughter Sam was beautiful and whole. She did not miss anything. I sighed and I felt relief. I thought I was the unhappiest woman on earth, and now I discovered that there were people that suffered more than me, and what impressed me the most was how they had overcome; that gave me more hopes. That man invited us to repeat some words that were going to change our life, and I didn't have any doubt to confess that I needed God, that I gave him my heart's keys to come in me and make me a new person, full of his love, joy, peace and kindness to guide me along my existence.

Since that moment, something happened. My temper was strong. I had addictions, a hard smoker, and hysteric, with a profane language, intolerant to my children, but especially to Samantha, who was really naughty, so I experienced that change they talked about.

MIRACLES

When getting home, it was something that I didn't understand. I just told my husband that I felt as light as a feather in the air, so my daughter came as usually dropping things, and I whispered to her, "keep quiet, my little daughter" with a soft voice. I couldn't shout. It was like someone had turned down my voice volume. Then, I realized that it wasn't necessary to yell or say rude things. And the most amazing is that after 6 months of going to the ladies' meetings, I stopped smoking. I suffered a lot because nobody smoked in the meetings, but there were ashtrays, and I did not dare to break the order and for what others may say, so when I got home, I smoked two or three cigarettes for the time I hadn't been able to smoke there.

I kept going because they spoke so beautifully in those meetings that I came back home with a great joy, and I recognized that I didn't want to smoke anymore. But in the past, I had made several attempts, and all of them failed. In the meetings, I was taught that I could talk with God, and have a personal relationship with him, as a Father and his daughter that he help us in everything, so I told him:

"Dear father, I don't want to dirt you anymore if you entered my heart, the smoke and nicotine is a dirty thing for the place where you dwell now. Help me, Lord as I have tried so many times and I haven't been able to do it"

Three days went by like that and I didn't take any cigarette, and the most impressive is that I carried cigarettes in my bag, my husband and sister smoked and I didn't feel like smoking one, not even one so far almost 20 years since then. WHAT A WONDERFUL MIRACLE!

PRAYER OF FAITH

Commitment
My Father
I ask you for forgiveness for all my sins
I repent from all the wrong I have done in my life.
I recognize that you died on the cross to pay all my sins.
I receive you today as my only Lord and Savior.
Be my guide in everything I do.
And write my name in the Book of Life
In the name of Jesus. So be it.

JOY IN THE MIDST OF REJECTION

So, Pamela was born in the middle of chaos in our life, many changes

of work

of city

of habits

of a new life in Jesus Christ.

She was a girl that had a very white skin and dark hair, with her very big and beautiful eyes, very long eyelashes. Wherever she went, "she would be admired". Besides being very beautiful, she was very good. She did not cry. Wherever you left her, she used to stay there without making any noise. She used to fall asleep in her walking aid. We were not able to buy things for her as we did with our first children. Now we were looking for a way to get ahead financially, so she used to wear good clothes, but they were presents from her older cousin, which did not fit her. They were difficult moments, but children do not suffer much at that age as adults do when we can't give them what we wish. Even so, she proved to be a different girl.

She didn't play with dolls or toys for her age. She wished to be at school with her brother. When I taught Abraham the multiplication tables, she was the one who learnt them by heart, and things like that. She entered school and all the children cried, she used to be calm, encouraging the others. She was outstanding in all the areas. One day, I checked her notebook, as I never used to do it. I was amazed that all her work and homework sheets had 100's as qualification, and a lot of pieces of advice from her teachers such as "How smart you are". "Keep like that and you're going to be a triumphant", "you are an example to follow", etc. I was amazed. I wasn't used to that, with a special daughter who didn't know how to grab a pencil and a son that suffered a lot to learn, and the most important, she learned to pray to God with me. She cried when feeling his presence and she used to say, "mom, why am crying like that when I pray?", and I answered, "It's the Holy Spirit who is touching you". I felt that God was giving to me a reward with this so different and special daughter. She has given to us a lot of satisfaction in primary school:

She was always in the List Honors

She was a Standard Bearer in the escort.

She was in the school music band

She represented her school in knowledge contests.

She was outstanding in everything.

At nine years old, she started to get fat in a strange way. It was evident. She cried, because she received bulling at home. Her brothers used to say offensive words such as "pig", "hog" "sow". You make me feel sick, and top of all, my husband worried me because he would give her to eat. We had arguments for that situation as she couldn't even have her normal meal due to his weight and body shape. I used to pray and cry with God, and asked him to help us.

One day I was sleeping, and when I got up, I listened clearly to a voice as a very strong thought, knowing that it was God… and said to me:

"If you don't treat her well, I will take her"

Being a God-fearing woman and fearful of those so direct thoughts that always gave me instructions. I cried the whole morning and talked to my son and my husband when she wasn't present, so that she couldn't get scared. I asked them to live hear alone, because I didn't want my daughter to die to go with God. Since that moment, they reacted and stopped afflicting her and me.

At school some children mocked at her body shape and she defended herself by saying:

"One day the little fat will go away, but your foolishness, I don't think it will".

And with academic achievements, she defended herself and she was respected.

At secondary school, she got the first place in achievement during 3 years. Besides that, their Class partners nominated her for an acknowledgement called, "FELLOWSHIP CUP" for being the girl who had the best friend relationship with everyone at school. A double acknowledgement for her life.

We used to thank God for all those so pleasant surprises.

At Preparatory School, she was outstanding, and at university, she got the first place during the four years of her major. The President's Office gave her a scholarship, and she was the Student Society's President over four years.

It's clearly written, "If you listen to these commands of the Lord, your God that I am giving to you today and you carefully obey them, the Lord will make you the head, not the tail, and you will always be on top, not at the bottom"   (Deuteronomy 28: 13)

Now I know that his promises are fulfilled, and her life has been successful. There was just an area in which she hasn't been fortunate, love.

Her friends with boyfriends since they were 15, and she only received rejection as from friends and from gallants. She was too robust and smart for the girls of her age, so she looked as their mom. During test periods, our house was full of male and female children who only used her to teach them and they could pass their tests. After that, they rejected her, didn't invite her to parties. They lied to her saying that they were not going, and my son used to pick her up and said, all "your friends" are there, so she cried a lot. One day that my husband and I cried out to God for her, and I felt inside my heart these words:

"The Lord says to not beg love, beautiful girl. He has reserved a gallant for you and is a foreigner". She got relief. We did too and hugged her.

At 20, God broke all the curse of not having a boyfriend in my daughter. (The foreigner has not come yet).

But she is very happy. She graduated as a BACHELOR OF ARTS IN INTERNATIONAL RELATIONSHIPS. She has got a job and is studying a master's degree, which she wants to complete en Europe.

"Two years ago she was living in Virginia USA about two years, she was working an studying fulfilling another of her dreams and overcome her fears".

Now she is working in an Institution for children with disabilities and she earned recognition as an employee of the year for the Glory of God!

I know that God does not fulfill nonsenses, but he does fulfills his purposes… and dreams…

THE LORD SAYS:

"I am the Lord, God of all the peoples of the world. Is there anything too difficult for me?"

Song for my daughter

My beautiful and sweet girl

The things of life
My beautiful and sweet daughter
You weren't in my plans
I cried out my misfortune
Without God I was
With vanity I filled up
You frustrated my career
My body you made shapeless
You came in a bad moment

According to me, I decided
About my own life

Plunged into depression
Jesus came into my life
Giving me revelation
Of all my evilness
That in his plans
You were even before
Being born and give me
Joy in the midst of
Pain, for so much
Suffering,
I couldn't deny it
Seeing you impacted me
Your beautiful black eyes
I couldn't resist
Besides, knowing
You might have died
I didn't recognize
Whom I really had
A sweet girl
A gift for my life
Every day you would give a proof
You weren't from this world
Your good behavior
Your great intelligence
Your great commitment to Christ
You were so different
From all the others.

I wasn't used to
Such a wonderful gift
You changed my sadness

Into all the opposite
And till today
You keep making it
Whatever you start over
There is always a blessing

Beloved King Jesus
For that I love you so much
Although I was so evil,
You focused you attention
In this unworthy servant
What she only does
Is serve you of emotion

You, you are really good

I LOVE YOU, MY JESUS!

6

THE JOY OF BEING FREE

OCCULTISM IN MY GENERATIONAL LIFE

My mother's family comes from a generation offspring of witchcraft, the tendency of telling ghost stories, was for that same reason.

I searched about this issue upon my mother's premature death and a sequence of deaths in our family. One year her great-grandmother passed away; then my mother; after her, her youngest brother and finally her second brother. (Her family was over).

Who was next now?

The next generation was us, "THE CHILDREN".

My mother dies at 35 years old. My uncle Berna die at 41 years old and my uncle Simon die at 50 years old" they were in a productive age.

What my grandmother's and great-grandmother's lives had been like, I learned about the story through an aunt, the oldest lady in my mother's family. My great-grandmother practiced occultism. It was said that they talked with dead or apparitions. She had an Estate that she had bought with a treasure that she had found. Another shocking thing is that she could say prayers backward and forward to make "owls" fall down, which are the birds the witches supposedly become. She used to order them to stop by her house next day for salt, and in effect, the ladies appeared in person as they used to go and ask for salt in person. My grandmother healed people and my mother used to sweep us with herbs and an egg when we were little.

Before getting married, we would go to a cousin on my mother's side, who was also involved in occultism, and for us, she was our god. Every problem that arose, we used to go with her to give us a solution with prayers and remedies.

One day we were invited to a spiritual retreat of my denomination. In that encounter, I recognized that that wasn't good and I asked God to forgive me. But I didn't know that it was necessary to do a generational deliverance.

I discovered about all this in Deuteronomy 18:9-14 in the Word of God.

"When you enter the land the LORD your God is giving you, be very careful not to imitate the detestable customs of the nations living there. For example, never sacrifice your son or daughter as a burnt offering. And do not let your people practice fortune-telling, or use sorcery, or interpret omens, or engage in witchcraft, or cast spells, or function as mediums or psychics, or call forth the spirits of the dead. Anyone who does these things is detestable to the LORD. It is because the other nations have done these detestable things that the LORD your God will drive them out ahead of you. But you must be blameless before the LORD your God. The nations you are about to displace consult sorcerers and fortune-tellers, but the LORD your God forbids you to do such things."

"Do not bow down to them nor worship them for I the Lord your God am a jealous God who does not tolerate you give your heart to other gods. I LAY THE SINS OF THE PARENTS UPON THEIR CHILDREN; THE ENTIRE FAMILY OF THOSE WHO REJECT ME IS AFFECTED-EVEN CHILDREN IN THE THIRD AND FOURTH GENERATION"

Therefore, I was released from all generational curse of witchcraft and occultism as well as my children, grandchildren and my great-grandchildren in a Leaders' meeting in Houston, TX.

It is important to know our story and pre-story. There are families with so many disgraces, and we don't understand why some failures, diseases, ruin, deaths, etc. occur

I wish with all my heart that all these experiences can help set you free and give your loved ones a better future.

It is like buying a ticket to our children to be happy.

AS IF WE DON'T CONFESS YOUR HIDDEN SINS AND GENERATIONAL CURSES, OUR CHILDREN WILL KEEP LIVING WITH THOSE CURSES.

If there was abandonment in your generations, you might suffer abandonment and your loved ones too. For that reason, there are many divorces in the world.

My grandmother got divorced from my grandfather for his adultery, and my mother and her little brothers were abandoned by them in their childhood. They lived with several relatives. For that reason my life was full of a lot of abandonment. The songs written by José-José I liked the most during my youth dealt a lot with abandonment.

"If you leave now"

"How sad everybody says I am".

"Don't tell me that you are leaving"

If there were violations, our children are going to be violated, and that terrifies me. We have to cover our children.

If your parents committed sexual immoralities as adultery, fornication, etc., our future generation will pay that bill and twice.

David committed adultery with one woman... his child Salomon sinned more. He had 700 wives and 300 concubines besides he adored other gods.

(1 King 11:3)

"Look, today I am giving you the choice between a blessing and a curse! Blessing, if you obey the commandments that I, the Lord your God that I am giving to you; curse, if you disobey the commandments of the Lord your God and turn away from the way that I am commanding you to follow, and go after gods that you have never known before".

(Deuteronomy 11:26-28)

In a book about Inter-generational healing, God revealed me that after an abortion, our womb remains with a curse, and the second child that occupies that womb, receives it. My daughter Samantha was the one who occupied my womb after that sin.

After God revealed by the Power of his Holy Spirit another curse through the names we give to our children. I found out that the name Samantha was borne by the first witch from Salem, who was burnt in the bonfire in the 17th century. Besides to honor her name, there is a sitcom about a witch that moved her nose, named Bewitched. We all laughed at her evilness. But witchcraft is real. I asked God to forgive me for my ignorance about and I covered my daughter with His precious blood. The most wonderful is that God baptized us with other names and my daughter was joyful to be given a new name by the Lord.

"PEARL OF JESUS".

PRAYER

Inter-generational Healing

Heavenly Father:

Today I come before you to ask you for forgiveness for all the sins committed by my ancestors in all my past generations and I break with any other pact made consciously or unconsciously with occultism and witchcraft. I cut out all adultery, sexual abuse, vices, divorces, single status, infertility, cancer, tumors, AIDS, hearth attacks, diabetes and other type of disease and any other abominable sin in my generational line and in my own life. Today I recognize you as my only God and Savior and receive your blessings. Since now, my future generations will be blessed through me and the decision of following you...

In the name of Jesus. Amen.

"If you obey the Lord your God in all and carefully comply with all his commands that I am giving to you today, the Lord your God will set you high above all the nations on earth". If you obey the Lord your God, you will receive the following blessings:

Your cities and fields
will be blessed
Your children and crops
will be blessed
The offspring of your herds and
*flocks will be bles*sed
Your fruit baskets and
breadboards
will be blessed
Wherever you go and whatever
you do,
you will be blessed.

»The lord will defeat your enemies when they attack you. They will attack you from one direction, but they will scatter from you in seven.

»The Lord will guarantee a blessing on everything you do and will fill your storehouses with grains. The Lord your God will bless you in the land he is giving to you.

»If you obey the commands of the Lord your God and walk in his ways, the Lord will establish you as his holy people such as he swore he would do. Then all the nations of the world will see that you are a people claimed by the Lord they will stand in awe of you.

»The Lord will give you prosperity in the land he swore your ancestors to give, he will bless you with many children, a great number of livestock and abundant crops. The Lord will send rain at the proper time from his endless treasury in heaven and will bless all the work you do. You will lend to many nations, but you will never need to borrow from them. (Deuteronomy 28:1-12)

7

THE JOY OF ACCEPTING A DAUGHTER OF SPECIAL NEEDS

I have experienced the joy of being mother and the pain of seeing my first daughter grow up differently from the others. Her childhood was quite normal until she was four years old, after she suffered her first convulsion. She stopped being interested in learning. She did not have the capacity of grabbing a pencil to write. I did not have any knowledge about what was happening with her life. Nobody told me that through this sickness she was going to suffer an intellectual disability. Not even doctors did it. She was very hyperactive and we went through a lot of anguish, danger when we used to go out with her, such as releasing my hand and being ran over by a car to getting lost in the stores, and going through an agony when I couldn't find her. One day, a friend took her out the men's restrooms.

I was always stressed out as I used to work and beside that I had marital problems; and due to my ignorance, I was really rude to her, and I verbally and physically mistreated her. I decided not to go out. I preferred not to socialize with anybody or to go to any place as I couldn't stand see people observe her as something rare, and with good reason, she was different. I continue feeling that God was punishing us, and that made me very unhappy. When she turned 8 years old, I decided to give my life, my children, my problems and my suffering to Christ, and something happened. First, I stopped being stressed out. I felt in peace and started to be patient with her.

Eventually, a female friend gave me away a poem about a father that had a special daughter and reading it touched my soul. As my thoughts started changing, what for me was a punishment, now I understood it was a God's gift, that we were chosen to be parents to this little angel, that my husband and I have being transformed to have the character and strength to be able to accept her, comprehend and love her as God sends it as "a combo", It was not only for us, but also for my children who were ashamed, especially, my second son Abraham, who did not invite little friends home for having a different little sister. I remembered that some school partners made a surprise visit to him. He was so worried that he started to yell at her little sister, crazy! Crazy! He did it earlier than the others mocked at her. Only God could transform their hearts and give them a great love for her. We take care of her as something really valuable, fragile and beautiful. We just feel gratitude for that great blessing.

Eigth years ago a serious situation happened to my daughter Samantha. She started convulsing every twenty minutes the whole night long and day. She was very weak; she couldn't walk or talk. For many years, she hadn't gotten so sick, neither when she got sick for the first time nor in her childhood. The maximum convulsions she had a day were sick. Since I meet Jesus, I gave him everything, my life, my family, the diseases, etc. I rested on him, and gave him control of everything. Now I didn't understand what was happening with my daughter. I prayed and I asked him to tell me "what for" this was happening, and he answered me in my heart with three questions:

1. **Silvia, do you love me**? And I as Peter, said. "Lord, you know everything, and you know that I love you". And he answers, "Do you love me more than you love Samantha?" And you know, I did tremble there! Because some days before I was observing my daughter, and I felt so much love for her that I made a question to myself. Shall I be loving her more than God? No, no, Lord, you are the first one in my life, but God who knows everything was asking the question because He already knew it. So, I recognized my weakness. I asked him for forgiveness, and I said to him, "*Help*

*me only to love you before loving her. I don't want
to offend you my Lord".*

2. *Are you willing to give your life for her*? And
I answered to him. "Of course, Lord, I am. What
mother wouldn't be willing to give her life for
a child? I just ask you to totally heal her, and
leave her whole body complete, so that she doesn't
suffer with anyone". Later, he kept silence all
early morning long. He didn't answered not matter
I talked to him. I went to The Bible to get an
answer, and I got nothing. I listened to a recording
of a conference from a Nicaraguan fellowship
leader on my cellphone, and I fell asleep. I just
wake up early and listen to the conference that
he tells me:

3. **Are you willing to give your daughter in
sacrifice as Abraham did it for love to my name?**
You know. I bent down there, I cried and said, "Are
you going to take her now, my Lord? Thank you for
letting me enjoy her for these 20 years, and it's going
to hurt me a lot, but she is yours. You gave her to
me and I totally give her to you. Thank you Lord",
and he answered to me, "a threefold cordon". We
were just looking for a hospital to take her. Her aunt,
who is a doctor came to see her and told us "if you
don't immediately place her in the hospital, she may
have a heart arrest or a stroke because she is very
weak". I talked with my family. I told my husband
and children what I had been talking with Jesus, and

I didn't know that my daughter was leaving now, and that they had to give her too and his will would be done.

They cried and God revealed me that the threefold cord was a family's prayer, that our prayer was not reinforced. Everyone was praying on their own, so we needed to do it as s family. She was in the hospital the convulsions were controlled for some hours, and she had convulsions again until the neurologists told us that they had to totally disconnect her as a computer and reset her again. They induced her in a comma. She was 16 days in the hospital. They administered tests in her whole body, many sleepless nights, but we had a lot of peace. We prayed together all those days and my son burst into crying and said. "Lord, don't take her. I was thinking that I want a car and branded clothing, pure nonsenses. I don't want anything, just my sister. Don't take here, please".

Honestly, we all did cry because we didn't know that he brought all that in his heart. So we found out about his purposes. He was making my son react, he had bad thoughts that made his existence bitter. After ten days of being disconnected, she was connected again and we were frightened again because she had pneumonia, because the tubes had damaged her inside. Her aunt told us not to worry, that it was normal and the infection would be removed with medicament.

THE BIGGEST MIRACLE THAT THE NEUROLOGISTS DIDN'T UNDERSTAND WAS SOMETHING THAT HAPPENED. HER BRAIN SHOULD HAVE BRAIN DAMAGE CAUSED FOR SO MANY CONVULSIONS FROM HER CHILDHOOD TO THOSE DAYS, AND THE MAGNETIC RESONANCE SHOWED THAT SHE HAD A NORMAL BRAIN AS ANYONE OF US.

They wanted to do more tests because they didn't understand it. We know that it was just one more proof of FAITH, and be able to see his power manifested in that BRAIN TO GIVE ALL THE ACKNOWLEDGMENT TO GOD. We brought her home. She didn't walk, didn't talk, and didn't eat. After some days, she started to give some little steps, to talk little by little and eat slowly. Her skin became brand new. The under eyes darkness she had since she was a little girl went away. She grew up some centimeters, and her bones were filled with flesh as she had a strange thinness. She came super intelligent. NOW SHE IS BEAUTIFUL AND FULL OF LIFE. She is still under medication because doctors say that she had a very little dose of medicament in her brain and for that reason she had convulsions.

We know that one single leaf from a tree doesn't move without the will of God. And we spiritually declare her 100% healed. She is 99% physically healed, and we know that God does not do things half-way, we expect that 1% of her total healing.

We GIVE thanks unto God for his immense mercy towards us and our daughter.

For that and much more, I made up a song for my beautiful daughter Sam.

"Angel from Heaven"

It is so wonderful
To have God with you
You see him everywhere
Let not be said in yours
God has given me the honor
For such a noble cause
Being mother to an angel
That has given home bright
It was not always like that

I wept my misfortune
Guilt-ridden I felt
For such imperfection
Looking for a solution
Without finding an answer
We had to look for you
Nothing was left
Just look at heaven
Beg for help
Without waiting
Your responses came
Giving me directions
That it was just a gift
That He has sent to us
Through her
He cleaned our heart
How dirty it was
Other thing he showed
In our weaknesses
His power is manifested
That it was just a deal
With our heart
That through it
He would give us salvation
It is so wonderful to have God with you
You see him everywhere let not be said
In yours.

PRECIOUS PEARL OF JESUS

WE LOVE YOU, LORD!

8

THE JOY OF BEING ABLE TO HELP

I supported all my siblings in whatever I could do, mostly, little women. I gave them their studies. I financed vocational studies to graduate as secretaries. Using my connections, I placed them in different banks.

My sister Norma is the fourth of my nine siblings. We have always gotten along well. She was the first one who graduated as secretary, she was just 15 years old. She is short and I made the terrible mistake of getting a birth certificate showing that she was 18 years old, just to have her work and help me get ahead my little siblings. I had her wear high heeled shoes, with make-up on, so that they believed she was that age (she could hardly walk). And as you reap as you sow, I paid a very high price for that mistake as I threw her at "the mouth of the wolf". She was really well shaped. Mature men started to prey. Parties prepared by clients for the bank employees came out, and they offered drinks. She used to get home very late. She became a very social person. Then, she bought a car and I didn't know where she used to go.

During that time women had being violated in my region and a girl had just been found abused and drowned. I couldn't stand more that worry, and I talked with God at my way, and I said that I gave her to him, to take care of her and that I had to be in peace and trusted in him.

Thank God nothing wrong happened to her. When she was 25, she made a mistake, having relationships with a friend, he wasn't her boyfriend. She got pregnant, and honestly, I respect her to date for "her courage" because she didn't care about what others might say, and being a single woman, she had her child Bryan. She was a big example for my life. She counted on our whole family's support to have her baby.

We had a short time walking in the ways of God, I had heard a testimony of a businessman that impacted me as he was a son to a single mother.

During this times, single mother issue was more marked, and he told how he was humiliated by her mother's family since he was a child. They did bullying at school because his mother gave him her last names as his father didn't want to recognize him as happened to my sister with her child's father.

Since Bryan was born, we loved him in my family as he lived together with my children a lot. I asked my sister and husband if my husband could give him his last name, so that he could not suffer "with just one last name", and both accepted. Bryan bears the same last name as my children. During that time, my sister gave her life into Jesus at the FGBMFI, and at the same time, she already had plans to go to the United States to work and come back to rebuild my mother's house and live with her little son there. She left and she came back soon. The boy had already turned about 3 years old, and I told her "You should start over your life, you are too young. Search for a dad for the boy now that he is little. He could love someone as his father". My sister said that it was in her plans. She dedicated too much time to her little boy and to work, and she had forgotten about her.

So my friends and I at FGBMFI started to pray for someone to come to her life, a good and hardworking man, and who loves her and her child, and God answered quickly. Approximately seven months later, his gallant Jim came. He was a very hardworking man, just as we asked God.

He treated her very well and her son and proposed marriage to her, and so they got married. He was divorced and had several children. She didn't matter because she had hers. They had a good marriage. He got along very well with her son, and everything was going just right till she got pregnant again. My nephew felt displaced, besides he entered adolescence, and he rebelled so much that he committed evil.

He was sent to a boot camp where he was behaving very well to come back to his mom on the weekend, when he was coming back home, my sister, who had problems with her husband, said to her that he couldn't receive him. My sister called to tell me that her son went back to the boot camp, and that she had been called and was told that her son had being crying the whole night, with a lot of pain, Then, he calls his mom to say goodbye because he was going to escape from there.

I prayed God for him, and I wasn't able to sleep during the whole night. He revealed me that he was going to commit suicide, he was saying goodbye to her mom and he was going to escape from life because her mother has turned her back on him. I intensively cried for him. I asked my husband to call to find out if he was fine. My husband called and he was told that he was in a class and he could call back in ten minutes.

He was asked who had called him, and my husband answered, "His dad from Mexico". After a while, we called again and he answered very happily. I think he thought it was his biological father, and my husband says, "I am your uncle, son", but I am legally your father in Mexico.

He got happy because all his friends and teachers were very impressed with the call from his "father" for the first time. My husband says, your Aunt Silvia is very worried about you and wants to talk to you. So he passes the call and I said to him, "Son, we want to help you. We are your family, you aren't alone. There's a home for you here. We love you". He said that he couldn't, that he had a trail, and he might not be permitted to leave the country, etc. "Please, let yourself be helped". And my husband took the phone and said to him "you want help or you don't, so we won't be losing time with this call!" And he responded yes. He wanted to come to our home.

My husband went to the citation with the judge, and we were praying so that he could be permitted to leave the country. God answered without any delay. The judge ruled on his favor. His teachers supported him for his good behavior, and my husband brought him to leave with us for a year. At home we treated him worthily. He came as a "cholo", with tattoos, shaven-headed, and XXL clothes. We bought clothes for him to dress well. He had a good haircut, and he is very well-educated, we didn't have so much trouble. Just one day that he went up the roof with a friend of my son, and we got scared. We thought that he was breaking in, so my husband gave him a strong rebuke. After this scolding, he was crying repented with me, and he brought with him a napkin with blood spot, and saw cuts in his wrists. I got scared and started praying to cancel all spirit of suicide.

And we gave him a lot of love and spiritual help. One day I asked him about that time we called him when God revealed me that he was going to take his life, and he confirmed me that he did do it. He took a bottle of pills, but he didn't die. They just took away his strength, and he couldn't rise, and he asked God for forgiveness for having attempted it.

WE INTRODUCED TO HIM HIS FATHER, WHO NEVER FAILS, OUR LORD JESUS CHRIST, AND HE GAVE HIS LIFE AND PLANS INTO HIM. HE CAME BACK INNERLY RESTORED, KNOWING THAT HE IS VERY WORTHY AND HE HAS A FAMILY THAT LOVES HIM.

I talked to my sister, and asked her son for forgiveness, for denying to receive him.

She came for him, and upon arriving, he asked my sister's husband for forgiveness. And his relationship with them was restored.

NOW HE IS A GOOD YOUNG MAN, WILLING TO BE SUCCESSFUL IN EVERYTHING HE UNDERTAKES. WE THANK GOD FOR BEING INSTRUMENTS OF HIS LOVE TO OTHERS.

"For I was hungry, and you gave me food; I was thirsty, and you gave me a drink; I was a stranger, and you took me in; I needed clothes, and you gave me clothing; I was sick, and you cared for me; I was in prison, and you visited me. (Mathew 25:35-36)

9

JOY BEFORE DEATH

MY FATHER

After forgiving my father and his wife, I had the joy of having a nice family relationship. I was always by his side every moment, caring for his needs and health. I used to visit him very often. I tried to talk to him about God, and he started to reject me. My husband told me to keep silence and not bother him, so I kept quiet about this topic, and one day his hand was hurt and bounded, and my daughter Pamela, who was just 5 years old, suggested him to say a prayer for his healing, and he didn't reject her as it seemed something very sweet for him in such a little girl. Next week that we visited him he was so amazed because his hand was completely healed-when you remain quiet, God uses the children. After he saw what happened, he started making questions to me about God and his Word until he was willing to open his heart and accept Jesus as the owner of his life.

Four years ago, very painful situations occurred in my family. One day I was called to tell me that my father was seriously sick in the hospital. He had suffer a liver burst due to a chronic cirrhosis and he had a short time left to live. As a woman of faith, I was very strong, but suddenly, I started to visualize myself in mourning, see the burial, and I began to cry as a little girl. Suddenly, I felt a very strong thought from God that said to me: "Wipe your tears away, your father is not dead. Even Lazarus who was dead for three days, I resuscitated him. Do you think I cannot raise your father?" I immediately wiped my tears away. I stopped crying believing what I had received in my thought, in a very strong manner it was God.

I went to the hospital next day. It was three hours away from my place of residence. All my brothers in the United States were already there. I came into the hospital room, and what I saw terrified me. He was so badly sick, that I felt like crying. He seemed to be dead. His skin pale without life, but I held back and I remembered what I had felt from God; those words that gave me hope. I prayed and cancelled all spirit of death and declared life on his unconscious body, and I asked God for new organs in the name of Jesus recognizing that he has the power to do everything new. Besides, I asked him to give my father longer life as King Hezekiah narrated in The Bible and for all the time we have been devoted to his service, my father will get healing. That day nothing happened, the doctors approached and they confirmed the diagnosis, and he was dying. I didn't accept it inside me and declared life.

Next day he continued without reacting, and I kept believing in those words and reading The Bible to him. In the afternoon, he suddenly begins to complain and I ask him. How are you, daddy? And he says, "Pretty bad". I was very happy because he was speaking very weakly. But every question I made to him, he answered it. Next day he had already opened his eyes and wanted to go to the bathroom, which he couldn't do of course. On the third day, he already had a beautiful color on his cheeks, sat asking for something to eat, and I said to him, "your "food is in the serum you're being given.

The fourth day he was already having some chicken broth, and walked to go to the bathroom. Right after that the doctors started to do tests because they didn't know what had happened with the dying patient. I came back home sure that GOD HAD MADE HIS MIRACLE as Lazarus'. So he was two precious years alive and healthy.

2012 was a very difficult year in my life. In the month of January I am told that he had fallen down and gotten a leg broken. He came back to the hospital and in a month he was going to be operated, and from the board he was sent back because his blood didn't coagulate, and he wouldn't resist the surgery. He was like that for more than three months with three attempts of surgery until we were told that if he went into surgery, he was going to die there. It was better to take him home and we would have him more time. So, in May of the same year, he became weak and didn't want to eat and everything bothered him. I was called to go to see him, and that night, I talked to God, and I felt the deepest pain to know that he was not going to give him more time. It was his time for leaving. Anyway, we helped him with doctors and medicament, but he didn't reacted anymore.

That day that he was agonizing, I had to serve a conference on principles and values in the United States, so I stayed with him all the time. I told my siblings to say goodbye to him. If it was necessary to forgive or ask for forgiveness, it was the right time. I also did it and asked him not to be afraid. I read for him about the place where he was going according to The Bible. He was surrounded by all his children, grandchildren and loved ones, and I told him, daddy if you could see how we are here, so many people saying goodbye, and The Bible says, that the time to say goodbye is better than your birthday, because when you are born, you come here to suffer and when you go back with GOD, is ENJOYING ETERNAL

LIFE; where you go, there is no sickness, you are going to be healthy and young, without worries. You deserve this goodbye because you were good, father, despite your mistakes. You deserve this goodbye, with all those that love you and thank God for this privilege as many die alone by themselves in a nursing home, and you have a good company". We all kissed him, and said these words to my brothers:

One day Jesus told a young man to follow him in his service.

The man accepted, but he said:

"Lord, first let me go back home and I will bury my father"

JESUS ANSWERS:

Let that dead bury their own dead, but you go and proclaim the Kingdom of God.

THEN HE INVITED ANOTHER ONE:

I will follow, Lord, but first let me say goodbye to my family.

JESUS ANSWERED:

Anyone who puts their hands to the plow and then looks back is not fit for the Kingdom of God

I say to my brothers, you are not dead, you already know Jesus. I am going to serve him and give that conference. Before going, I cried out at a loud voice...

LORD JESUS, RAISE HIM OR TAKE HIM WITH YOU!

YOU RAISED HIM ONCE. I KNOW YOU CAN DO IT AGAIN!

I left, and when I was half of my way, my sister called me to tell me that twenty-minutes ago my father has just left. I told her, little sister, don't cry, GOD ANSWERED MY PRAYER. HE DECIDED HE MUST BE WITH HIM. HE ALREADY RESTED FROM HIS AGONY AND SUFFERING, WE ARE GOING TO REPOSE FROM SEEING HIM SUFFER. THERE CAN'T BE THE LEAST DOUBT FOR ME, JESUS CAME FOR HIM...

So a SUPERNATURAL PEACE came upon me that I got amazed and started singing God thanking him for giving to me such a wonderful father, and letting him live for 76 years in this world, being there for him till the last moment.

I imparted the conference; my friends couldn't believe that I was so calm and relieved. I think that they were more affected by the news, and mostly, of seeing me working for God.

I came back home at night. I searched for him in the funeral rooms, and he looked so nice like sleeping with such a peace, and his black shirt with little rosters because he liked chickens, hens and rosters very much. Right there I manifested my fondness, at the church, my sister and step-mother forgave each other.

HOW NICE GOD IS, HE WORKS IN OUR RECONCILIATION EVEN IN THOSE MOMENTS

- ❖ A piece of advice for every person that has lost a loved one, it is not good to be talking with them. It's is a need to let them rest. I listened to a story of a spiritual leader, which left me a great teaching.
- ❖ "His father died and he couldn't forget him. He missed him and used to talk to him every moment knowing that it was wrong. One day he decided not to cause more hurt to himself, and asked God for forgiveness for retaining him, and he said, I give him in your arms, Lord. He doesn't belong to this world anymore. Suddenly his room door opens, and it was his father telling him, "Thank you son for letting me go.
- ❖ I set a picture of my father on my computer screen after he passed away. Every time I turned it on, I used to talk to him and express my fondness. After that message I understood that I had to let him rest.

My mother-in-law

My great friend; since I became her son's girlfriend, she treated me very well. She admired me very much for the courage that God had given to me to bear suffering, so since that very moment, she rebuked my husband to not let me lose time if he wasn't thinking of something serious with me.

She was an admirable woman, with a strong character, but very positive. She was a warrior for her family, a very hard-working woman making her family going over any situation. She was very generous. She retired as a nurse, and people love her for her support and goodness. She took time to be with his children and grandchildren. She was my great support when my daughter Sam was born. She even used to blame herself for my daughter's disease for all the sins that she committed in her life, and it made her suffer that she got sick and that people were so cruel at looking at her granddaughter through bad eyes. She couldn't overcome that. I used to ask her not to worry, and bless them. Regarding her mistakes, I used to encourage her by always telling her that "God had already forgiven her, and if her sin were red like scarlet, he would make them white as wool". She finally could release herself from family secrets and she consciously received Jesus. When I had to travel, my children stayed cared for her. In the end, their grandmother treated them better than I did. I found my house "really clean". She was so neat. An example of woman!

ALZHEIMER

Approximately at 70, she started to have a lot of fears in her house. She got really depressed and cried a lot in the afternoons, so we hosted her every night. For about 8 years she was in my house like that, so that she didn't feel alone. Later, forgetfulness started. She was clinically declared with Alzheimer. Now she couldn't be alone and we had to talk about that as a family and hosted her for one year with a niece, his youngest son and us. This disease deteriorated her every day. She repeated the same things and told stories about her childhood, and as the symptoms increased, she invented lies, besides, her legs didn't respond. It was a very hard time that the family was affected. She forgot to change her clothes or take a shower. I used to say, I am going to take care of your dignity while you are with me, so I colored her hair, put on lipstick on her lips and enamel on her nails. She got smartly dressed by me. She called me "Chivis" and used to say, "Now you are my mom".

One friend asked me one day: "Mrs. Silvia, why do you take care of your mother-in-law? This disease wears away much more people who take care of them than they who are sick. I had my mother like that for 10 years and it's a progressive disease. Now it only remains that she gets violent, naked and leaves home with no direction. She must face this sickness with her daughters who are the only ones that can stand this hard disease, because that has caused some elders to be mistreated".

I answered to her that her daughters lived in the United States, and they worked and weren't able to take care of her.

My friend was so right. As time went by, she started to become more aggressive. The only one she hit was the girl that helped me. She already had some frictions with me. In spite of everything, she did not openly insult me. I told her to respect me that I just wanted her to be well. When she left home and another child took care of her, she only said lies, such as I didn't give her to eat, I didn't want to take her out of home because I was ashamed of her, that we treated her badly and she used to say negative things about the person who took care of her.

We had to talk as a family to find out about her disease progress and affectations, and be careful of not believing what the disease invented in her brain. She always cried. One day she got desperate at home and said, "I am going to commit suicide if you don't take me home". I answered, "If you commit suicide, God won't receive you in heaven and you will go to other place, a very ugly one". She stopped, because she believed in God very much. Anyway, we used to keep an eye on her, so that she didn't attempt anything.

She had to be given medication, so she weren't depressed or uneasy. I think God was kindly to her and us. He didn't let her go to the following stages. One day my husband felt that we should have taken her to her home in Rio Bravo, something that she always wished in her heart, die in her home. We picked her at her niece's, the doctor, and took her home with my brother in-law. On our way home, I felt I should have prayed for her and feeling that we were not going to see her anymore. I didn't say anything to my husband to not scare him. We said goodbye to her. She cried and gave her son her blessing. Next day my husband had to make a trip to several countries in Central America. At the same time, I was invited to Honduras to give a conference with the FGBMFI Ladies. The banner was about Ruth and

Naomi (mother-in-law and daughter- in-law). When preparing the material, I realized about the precious relationship I had with my mother-in-law, and that afternoon, I honored her at the Convention, and in the evening, my husband calls me telling me that his mom is seriously sick, that he had to come back and I say to him.

"A child's responsibility is taking care of his parents, give them love, attention, resources, when they are alive as the poet said. I said to him that he had honored his mom. He assisted her, gave her his time and his care, and I asked him to remind what I did when my father was agonizing, to let the dead bury their dead (my sisters in-law also know about God) but if your pain is so big that you can't bear it, go, honey to see if you reach her alive.

I came back from Honduras the following day in the afternoon, and my children gave the news that her grandma had passed away at dawn. I immediately call my husband to find out how he was doing and if he had been able to find a flight to come back, and I find him sad and with weeping, and tells me about such a supernatural experience he had at dawn. His mother went to visit him and say goodbye to him. He saw her with a big smile and pretty young accompanied by his grandma. He told me if he hadn't had that experience, he wouldn't have believed anyone about this kind of visit. That right moment he understood that his mother knew that he wasn't going to be able to see her again, and God allowed her to go to say goodbye to his son.

When you have that connection with the WONDERFUL GOD even in your hardest moments, he gives you the satisfaction of giving your beloved ones to him hoping that one day we will see them again.

- WE LOVE HER AND I KNOW THAT SHE IS ENJOYING IN THE PRESENCE OF GOD, AS SHE WISHED.

10

JOY DOES NOT DEPEND ON YOUR PHYSICAL BEAUTY

Since I was born it was said that I was a beautiful baby and kind of robust. My aunt Carmen (my godmother) gave me love. She said that I had such a smooth skin that she could be always touching me. I bear this name thank to her. My parents wanted to name me Clara. As I grew up, I was losing weight. In my adolescence I became a Barbie and later on I was medium sized. As I narrated before, I took refuge in my pride when my mother passed away. But I know that I wasn't ugly. Besides I acquired a very good body shape, very well-built that made draw attention.

I found myself discovering that my attributes were those that helped get advantages of some situations. In fact. When I became my husband's girlfriend, he told me that what he liked of me the most was my physical beauty.

When I graduate from my vocational program, I get a job as a cashier in a spare parts store. I was surrounded by metals and bolts. Not a very feminine place. One day a very well dressed person came to buy a spare part. Then he gave me a business card and invited me to a job interview to enter a bank. My boss who was a good person gave me permission and said that he "wanted me to prosper". I had an interview and a psychometric test, and I was hired. One day I found the interview in the personnel file, and the interviewer wrote an extra annotation that read "AND SHE IS VERY GOOD LOOKING", so that made my self-esteem got high, since that very right moment, my life changed. I had to dress well, started by putting on more make-up to highlight my beauty. I also began to color my hair and take care of my body shape as they made us wear uniform and sent several changes for a year. Vanity came to my life, plus the pride I already had. So, I started to lift another god on my life besides my job, MY BODY.

Everyone around me used to admire me. I only heard compliments towards me. I eventually became as the witch in the story telling Snow Flakes. I always had a mirror in front of me to be able to see myself, and asked it, "Little mirror who is the most beautiful?", and I believed that it answered to me "You are the most beautiful". I used to set fashions, and when I had my children, I became a diet slave. I used to gain a little weight, but I turned to my normal weight. I went on starvation diets. I used to say "If I want, I gain weight and if I want, I lose weight". For that reason, **I believed myself the god of my own body**.

When my husband was jealous of me, **he would make my self-esteem go down** by inventing stories about people. He ignored me no matter how much I got all dolled up for him. He stopped being nice to me. When I asked him for divorce, he asked for a new opportunity, and I accepted it thinking of what others might say. He said that he started to repeat to himself. Ï don't feel anything for her" until he truly came to not feel anything for me. For that reason, he ignored me. I enjoyed my job. There I felt admired, but in that house, I had my worst enemy, so I exaggerated much more my dressing style. I wore tighter clothing. It wasn't anymore to be admired by my husband, but to be admired by the others, and I started to get all dolled up for the people.

I remember one day I wore a top and tight jeans. I was almost violated in the street for being so provocative. I repented and stopped dressing like that as I got scared. When I get to know God, I start realizing that I cannot wear clothes like that. It wasn't pleasant for God. I had to be more decorous, and I started to dress better. When my husband and we forgave each other, he started to win my heart, and say beautiful things to me. I didn't need to exaggerate my beauty. He raised my self-esteem with so many nice things.

When I turned 39 years old, I started to feel strange. Suddenly, I felt a terrible anxiety, and I didn't know why. Then I started to feel intense heats in my neck and tachycardia, tiredness, uncontrollable cry, bone pain, brain pain, anger, change of mood, etc. I saw it was necessary to visit a gynecologist, and he made a hormone check test, which resulted normal. But observing that I had a lot of symptoms, he prescribed a milligram of estrogen, but it didn't cause contradictions, of what was going to happen. Six months later, I started to get exaggeratedly fat. I looked as a big ball.

A lot of volume on my face, volume in my arms, my breast, my stomach, the legs. Wherever I went, they got shocked and told me what happened to you, you are really fat! My husband said your body is becoming really rare. Of course, everything affected me and I got depressed, so I said to my husband, honey, what do you prefer, a beautiful body or a beautiful mood? And he answers, "I prefer a good mood" "I don't care about your body shape. Now I enjoy everything with you, you are my friend, my wife and my lover. I don't desire anyone else than you".

Look, I believed those words and they made me feel THE MOST BEAUTIFUL WOMAN IN THIS WORLD! I felt like I was a Barbie doll, now that I was like Barney. When I was like a Miss Mexico, he never treated me like now. In fact, when I refused to be with him in intimacy during the time I was in a really good shape, he used to say to me "what a waste".

MY FRIENDS, THE BEST PLASTIC SURGERY A WOMAN COULD EVER HAVE IS... A HUSBAND WHO TREATS US AS A QUEEN. WE GET REJUVENATED AND WE BECOME REALLY BEAUTIFUL. IT DOESN'T MATTER YOUR WEIGHT!

MY HUSBAND'S LOVE IS NOT BASED ON MY PHYSICAL APPEARANCE ANYMORE, BUT ON WHAT IS WORTHIER, INNER BEAUTY AND HAVING JESUS AS THE CENTER OF OUR LIFE

One day I began to feel a pain in my arm, and for that reason, I went to the endocrinologist. I was weighted and he said you are reaching obesity range, and I said, **"I know doctor, but I am a happy little plum!** And he said I had to care of me, so my heart and diseases don't attack me. I followed his instructions and he sent me to a nutritionist, who gave me a nutrition plan and I lost 10 kilos in three months. Honestly, I didn't like myself much for my age. I felt like my skin was going down. When my husband sees me tells me, "I don't like you are losing so much weight". Honestly, I laughed because it's admirable what God does in people's heart. I have gained a little weight to be able to please my husband.

GOD HAS BEEN GOOD AND DOES SO MANY CHANGES IN OUR HEART. NOW WE APPRECIATE WHAT TRULY WORTHY IS.

"I HAVE LEARNED HOW TO BE CONTENT WHATEVER I HAVE"   (Philippians 4:11)

"INNER BEAUTY COMES FROM A GRATEFUL HEART BECAUSE HE HAS MADE GREAT CHANGES IN LIFE".

11

TAKING ROLES THAT
AREN'T OURS

According to Erick Berne's Model, a Psychoanalyst
Medical Doctor,

We come to this world in a good condition "we all are born well". "We are all born princes and princesses". After our social intercourse with the others, we take self-limiting decisions through which we become "enchanted toads or frogs".

THE STATES AS PARENT-ADULT-CHILD EGOS

A. In my own life, I have been able to realize that I had to mature being a teenager, and take a role that wasn't mine, instead of being a sister, being a FATHER-(MOTHER)-ADULT by becoming head of the household head as my father granted me the rights to decide and take control of my house (economic and moral control).

My attitudes:

SERIOUS

AUTHORATIVE

RESPONSIBLE

MISTRUSTFUL

DETERMINED

PROTECTIVE

PROVIDER

THE STATE AS A <u>CHILD EGO</u>

I couldn't afford that luxury. There was no time for that. I loved so much my siblings. I used to cry for them, and I stood up thinking of them, but I never demonstrated with love, just with moral and economic support. I imposed them punishments if they behave badly, and if they behaved well, I used to give them just material presents. How could I be able to give love if I didn't have it?

My brothers grew up and went to the United States. Some of them got married. One day they heard that my daughter had been diagnosed with "Epilepsy", and convulsions had started. **"How good. God is punishing her because she was very bad at us"**. I got so surprised and got sad at the same time, and I made the following comment:

"The only thing I did was loving them, get them educated, and provide them with a roof, food and clothes. They were the very best for me, the driving force of my existence". That what was I felt for them. They were my world, and I truly loved them, and defended them against anything, but I made a terrible mistake. I NEVER TOLD THEM ABOUT IT OR DEMONSTRATED TO THEM.

Now I had to mend that mistake that I made with them. I recognized that it was true. I repented from what I did. I asked God for forgiveness, and the next step was going to Kansas, ask them for forgiveness and heal their hearts.

Coincidentally, my brother Ricardo, the youngest one of the males, was about to get married, so we went to his wedding. Our whole family got together, and in the end, the new married couple "supposedly" went on their honey moon trip. My father and his wife were with us at my sister's house, and next day in the evening, I told my sister Norma about my plan, but I got happy inside because things didn't happen, and I said, "It's too late now and tomorrow I'm going to Mexico; besides, Ricardo went on his honey moon. Well, I wanted to ask for forgiveness, but things simply hasn't happened yet". Approximately half an hour later, one of my brothers arrive, the one who made the negative comment about my punishment; then my older brother arrives with his family, and I hadn't understood yet. In fact, it is not easy to ask for forgiveness, and I thought that I had already been released.

BE CAREFUL ABOUT WHAT YOU PROMISE TO GOD, BECAUSE HE MAKES US FULFILL A PROMISE! SURPRISE!

Those that should be on their honey moon trip arrive.

What any other sign I needed to take the step... Nothing, just do it!

So I said to my husband, pray for me, I had to talk with all of them, and with fear and shame, I dared to ask for forgiveness to each one for not demonstrating my love and for just giving them material things and hardly disciplining them. I asked my father for forgiveness for judging him for so long time, for getting married, and his wife preempted, and asked for forgiveness for having married my father. I said, in the contrary, thank you for having taken care of my daddy and giving him your love and company at his mature age. That became an atmosphere full of forgiveness and tears.

My brother Pablo (older of my brothers) spoke in the name of all, and crying he said that they had nothing to forgive. They only had gratitude to me in their heart, and to my husband for always having sheltered and supported them in their worst situations.

My father placed his hand on his heart to see such a beautiful as well as strong scene. We were like children again having reconciliation with God and making our hearts get closer in unity and love, and thanking God for what he had done in our lives despite all kind of suffering, we were more united as never before. Till today.

THE STATE OF "CHILD EGO" IN MY LIFE HAS DEVELOPED THROUGH TEARS, HAVING TO BECOME AS CHILDREN ACTING AS SUCH WITH MY DAUGHTER SAM, I SING, DANCE AND PLAY WITH HER.

Honestly there is much left for me. THE BIBLE SAYS "WE HAVE TO BECOME CHILDREN TO ENTER INTO THE KINGDOM OF HEAVENS".

B. In my husband's life, THE STATE OF A CHILD EGO increased due to the experience in his childhood. He lived next to his maternal grandparents. He didn't meet this father, grew up with physical and psychological mistreatment, frustrated for not being able to play with his presents. He could just see them, not play with them. He lived wishing to be with his mother and it became true until he was 12 years old.

The state of ADULT EGO did not fully develop in his life, so from that time to today, I feel **"mom"** to everyone including my husband by providing what was missing in his childhood, in all his emotional life.

There was a time when he granted his rights to me when he went to work out of the city, and I took care of my children, the house and expenses. He only used to send me a check and I had to manage to find the way to stretch that money as far as possible. Being in charge was so good to me that when he come home and wanted to give his opinion about something, I asked him to be quiet telling that he knew nothing about what was going on, and he couldn't give any opinion. I was disrespectful to him, it didn't help him much, so that he could be the PARENT OR ADULT EGO".

After being taught in the word, I found out about my incompetence as a wife. I had to stop being a mother to take my place and give him his role OF THE HEAD OF THE HOUSEHOLD AND PRIEST OF MY HOME.

I STOPPED BEING THE WRONG HELPER TO BECOME HIS RIGHT HELPER.

It was very difficult for me to let him be my provider here on earth as I was used to make my own money through my job. Since he was a student, I already made a good wage. I gave everybody good presents. I used to lend to others and I didn't have to ask anything to anybody. I didn't work anymore and had to give him his place as the head of the household and priest of my home. I had to die to self. It was terribly hard for me to ask money for the expenditures. God was bending my pride, and it cost tears for me to submit to the authority imposed by God in my life. I also learned to keep quiet. I learned in the Proverbs.

"It is better to live alone in the corner of an attic than with a quarrelsome woman in a lovely home"

(Prov. 21:9)

For my transformation and obedience, God made "THE ADULT AND FATHER EGOS" grow in my husband, and I have given him his place in everything.

The word "EZER" in Hebrew means "HELP". This name is given to the wife.

The Bible says: "It is not good for the man to be alone, I will make a helper who is just right". Now I have appropriated this promise, and I support my husband, interceding for him and giving to him encouraging words, so that he goes ahead in his call of service; thus now I AM HIS HELP, HIS PROPHET AND

INTERCESSOR. I AM THE POWER BEHIND THE THRONE.

C. In my daughter Pamela's life, THE STATE OF "ADULT EGO" WASN'T THROUGH ANY EXPERIENCE. GOD DESIGNED HER A MATURE PERSON SINCE SHE WAS BORN.

Her personality since she was a girl was like that. She didn't play with dolls. She was very independent, her dreams and desires were entering school, studying and studying when I practiced the multiplication tables with Abraham, she learned them faster than him. She got bored during her long vacation because she wanted to go to school. I used to say, "Honey you aren't a normal girl" that's why she didn't fit the girls of her age. To date she is very mature in everything.

D. In some friends' life, I have seen other behaviors according to their life in their childhood and marriage. My friend "Maria" in her childhood had a permissive father and very protective, she became a girlfriend in her adolescence with one friend of her brothers, kind of older than her; and just as her father dies, she gets married to him, and since that very moment, **she adopted a husband as a father**, providing him with discipline and protection. She developed the "CHILD EGO" STATE.

E. Our friend Osiel is a so protective man, because during his childhood he had to **ADOPT THE**

ADULT EGO due to the prolonged absence of his father. Besides, a strong character was formed inside him for the bullying received in his childhood and for alopecia in his youth; and his wife **ADOPTED THE "ÇHILD EGO",** she sees him as a father and depends on him in a way that just thinking of the fact that he might not be there, she feels afraid of not knowing what to do.

So I have found out about similar stories in different roles. For that reason, I engaged in the task of researching this psychological phenomenon to look for **<u>a balance in this life</u>**.

12

THE JOY OF FULFILLING AS WIFE IN INTIMACY

My courtship lasted seven years, too much time, for reasons out of our control, my husband's major. Then he didn't find a job related to his profession. He went some time to the United States and worked as support for a contractor just to buy an engagement ring for me.

The Bible says:

So I say to those who are single and to widows: it is better to stay unmarried, just as I am. But if you can't control yourselves, you should get married. <u>It is better to get married than to burn with lust</u>.

(1Cor. 7:8)

I didn't consider myself a bad person. The thing is that my father gave me a lot of freedom or better said, I felt free to decide about my life. As I was of lawful age, I didn't ask for permission. I just let him know where I was going. Therefore, nobody forced me to do anything. It was voluntarily, because the flesh is weak, and we had sexual relationships before marriage in a time when such situation was unthinkable in a decent home. That sin took us to commit other sin, even bigger, "an abortion". Of course, I didn't know anything about cares to prevent pregnancy. I didn't have anybody to give me any advice. I didn't know if I was innocent or if it was convenient for me to believe that my period was late. A friend from my childhood, who had already had a similar experience, advised me to jump, hit my stomach, and take homemade remedies and nothing worked. Then she advised that I should go to a place and have a curettage or an abortion. Honestly, I got very much scared, but I couldn't afford to have a baby. At home, I was an example of daughter to my father and siblings. Besides that, I used to work in a public place and I might have even lost my job after many years of working there.

It is a very heavy burden not to forgive yourself for what you did, such intense physical and emotional pain, feel that you are dirty, evil and hypocrite. I kept living my life like that. The following year, my husband got a job. I had my wedding dress made. I wasn't able to make it white because I wasn't pure. It was made in ancient beige, because it was fashionable, but I know that it was to hide my sin.

As there were many children in my home, I didn't want my dress to get dirty. I abandoned my family. I went to my mother in law's house, so that they could help me get dressed. I paid the high price for what I did. I recognized my mistake of not staying with my beloved ones in such important moment. I was the first one that went for a hairstyle, and when I came back there was no one from my husband's family, but the maid. They had also gone for a hairstyle. I paid my mistake in that manner asking a girl to help me zip my dress and in my personal care. That was my first sadness. The second one was that I got to church expecting to see it full of flowers, and surprise, my uncle that had accepted to pay the flowers of the church forgot my wedding, so I got married crying for the flowers.

So many guests attended the wedding, I was very happy because my boyfriend had already complied with getting married to me. Thus, everything was really nice, but when we were alone, there was always that memory of what we had done last summer. No matter how much you mask things it is so deep that your life is always afflicted. After those two beautiful years of honey moon against all odds until my first daughter was born. I myself decided to plan that pregnancy, not God.

After my first daughter was born my husband changed. He became very jealous and made my existence bitter. He could psychologically treat me very badly the whole day long, and at night, jealousy and everything was gone; and in my bedroom, he was another man, trying to touch me, and I rejected him; just resentment, grudge and lack of forgiveness I had for him in my heart. Many times I almost had forced sexual relations, just to fulfill as wife. I got to be afraid of night to come and get into my room just thinking that my executioner was there. He sometimes used to say, "What is wrong with you, you are very hard" And due to my pride, I didn't answer anything. I just stored everything in my heart, and from those times I didn't want to be with him, my two Children Abraham and Pamela, children who weren't born from love, but from a relation to fulfill as a wife. I sometimes used to think to myself, why he didn't find a woman to leave me alone and not bother me. Imagine, what a nonsense! It is good that God never listened to me.

So we sometimes bring children that are born just to fulfill as wives, that is to say to procreate. Until I decided to forgive my husband since I was interested in my daughter's healing. I was able to truly feel what being healed from any wound is. I thought that it didn't exist, that it was religiosity, now I AM A WITNESS THAT GOD IS REAL IN MY LIFE AND THAT HE DOES HELP US IN ANY MOMENT.

After that forgiveness, I was able to see my husband through other eyes, full of LOVE, not mine, but FROM GOD. He conquered me again, and through a Conference that I prepared to release women in the sexual area, the first one to be released was me. I was released from taboos, from traditions that sex is dirty, etc. Now I understood that everything is so clear in The Bible.

"Don't let anyone capture you with empty philosophies and high-sounding nonsense that come from human thinking and from the spiritual powers of this world, rather from Christ". 		(Colossians 2:8)

Regarding the physical part, we have bodies that are composed of:

SEXUALITY AND CAPACITY TO REPRODUCE, "that man leaves his father and mother and joins to his wife, and the two are united into one".
						(Genesis 2:24)

THEY WERE NAKED AND DIDN'T FEEL ASHAMED.

How many times I was in intimacy with my husband and I felt ashamed that he saw me naked. Honestly, I didn't enjoy my sexual life thinking that it was for the mistakes I had made and lack of peace. I learned that God wanted us to enjoy each other, and not only fulfill as wife without feeling anything.

That God wanted our physical as well as our spiritual pleasure, approving mutual satisfaction. What he is not pleased with is sexual relations outside of marriage.

GOD IN HIS MARVELOUS CREATION PERFECTLY DESIGNED US WITH ORGANS AND SENSES TO MUTUALLY ENJOY EACH OTHER.

Salomon wrote about his beloved in Salomon's Songs of Songs:

How beautiful you are, how pleasing you are, my love, with your delights!

Your stature is like a palm tree, and your breaths like its clusters of fruits.

I said to myself: I will climb that palm tree, I will take its fruit.

May be your breasts be like grape clusters, the perfume of your breath like apples, your mouth like the best wine!

She might make the wine go straight. Flowing slowing over her lips

Of those who sleep. I belong to my beloved one,

And his desire is for me.

Oh, come my beloved, let us go to the countryside,

Let us spend the night in the villages.

Based on that learning I was another woman, I asked God for forgiveness for my mistakes from the past, and he release me. I felt his forgiveness and love. He gave me a new opportunity to make our marriage works. I asked him to help me cooperate in everything and understand...

THAT SEXUAL LIFE IS 70% IMPORTANT IN MARRIAGES TO BE ABLE TO BE HAPPY... A 30% IS ALL THE REST.

I asked for forgiveness for the time we lost and for depriving so much of sexual relations, for offering him in my heart to other women. I learned that we must communicate everything we feel even if for a moment you abstain from relations, and don't let it be for too long except they are moments to be with God.

From then on we practice **putting in God's hands our intimate relationship** as God is in every place even at that moment he give us his blessings.

13

JOY IN THE SERVICE OF GOD

Since I met Jesus and gave him my life, I truly fell in love with him.

I learned to talk with him as my father and I stopped saying pre-elaborated prayers that didn't have power in my life. Now I was telling him my sorrows, my dreams, my wishes, and I could feel his answers through his presence of LOVE, so inexplicable in my life that I broke down and cried. For me, it was something new, and I started to rejoice and find out that he was real and not an invention. I had already had an experience with Jesus in my denomination, and it helped me a lot, but my life didn't change. I was in a Bible study circle and read The Bible, but I didn't understand it and got bored, in fact, I used to sleep.

So, when I come into FGBMFI, and he is presented to me in a simple and practical manner through testimonies of power, I start to feel the presence of the Holy Spirit who I didn't know either. HE IMPRESSED ME! He removed my blindfold from my eyes and started to reveal me about the areas that were wrong. Now I could understand his word. I became hunger to learn more and more. My friends used to tell me that I wanted to run when I was a spiritual baby that I had to drink milk; then something more solid as mash to then understand that everything had a time. Even though, I prayed, fasted, read The Bible, listened to a Christian Radio. I learned that his word says:

"So faith comes from hearing, that is, hearing the good News about Christ".   (Romans 10:17)

My first experience about people seeing something in me (now I know that it was His light) was when a guest went to the meeting. She was a teacher, got closer to me and said to me, "Can I go to your house and talk to you? You made me feel very confident". I couldn't say no, but I was scared. I didn't know what piece of advice I was going to give to her, and I said inside my thought "Why didn't I tell someone with some more experience?" However, I got home and told my husband about it. I went to pray and I said to God, "I don't know what to do, help me, please". The teacher finally came and she started to tell me all her problems, and I just listened and listened. At the end, she says thank you for listening to me; talking with you was very good to me. I got more surprised than she was, and I understood that I something in me, God was using me to place me in his service, which WAS LISTENING TO THE AFFLICTED.

The partners with longer time taught me. I wanted my family to know him. Some rejected me starting with my family. My sisters got together and didn't invite me. It hurt me. Also my friend turned down on me. Nobody invited me to any social event. It did hurt, but I finally overcome. One day I wanted to take my oldest sister as a guest, and since her husband was very special and wouldn't let her go out, I invented a lie, so that she can tell to her husband and go with me. I thank God for the most experienced ladies in God's way, who corrected me about LYING, and she said, "If it is through lies, it is better that she doesn't come". I felt so ashamed, and right there, I realized that it was a life style that I had, "white lies". Since that moment, **I decided to change**, and not to say lies, and if I ever fail before him, he immediately convinces me from sin and corrects me.

"For the Lord disciplines those who he loves"

Then, I prayed for people and there were healings, miracles and releases. God started to use me his power just as he used my partner to correct me from my wrong way. Now I had a spiritual jealousy even in God's services there are some difficulties. A competence for the leadership started. It was a very big struggle. When the true vision of FGBMFI. Religiosity was removed. Most of the ancient ladies went away and only four women with me remained, who knelt asked God for new ladies to come. At that time. My partner also went away. Over time, that group was raised again and became full of women. Most people would go to me to pray for their needs as it was a new generation and the rest didn't feel capable to do it.

The leader that was jealous of me came back. The only thing she did was talking to everybody breaking the order. Some time later, I started to feel bad for pre-menopause symptoms, a lot of tiredness, and I asked them if someone could support me. Nobody wanted to take control, and she said that she would help me with the group. I wasn't leaving the group, just that this responsibility came a burden due to my health. She took control and since that moment she became my enemy. She didn't take me into account. If I gave an opinion, she would ignored me. She changed the rules at her will. I always came back home very upset and used to tell my husband about it. One day my husband tells me, "don't go anymore, you always come very affected, and like that you can't be a blessing to anybody". He was so right! I cried and in December I left.

I went like Jesus through the Way of Cross, for the women to whom I was given my time and my resources, for going to pray for them and their families even at night I left my children to go where they asked me to go. Suddenly, nobody remembered me. I felt abandoned, forgotten not even my best friend looked for me. I cried, I cried a lot. I felt betrayed, abandoned and forgotten. In February, on Valentine's Day, I herd on a Christian radio, if you have an enemy it's time to make it your friend in the name of Jesus; take the telephone, call her and ask for forgiveness. The truth I didn't call her. I called a flower store, and I sent to her a bouquet of flowers with a card in which I asked her for forgiveness for all I have bothered her. That same night there was an event of married couples of FGBMFI, I said hello to her, we kissed each other and she commented, "I liked very much what you sent me" and said, "We'll talk latter". I was very glad as she had already forgiven me, but it wasn't like that. She didn't speak to me for four years. I did my part. I know that it had nothing to do with me now, but her and her relationship with God, Even so I stayed home depressed for some time, because I couldn't seve him. It happened that God talked to me through a song which said to me, "You must become less, so I can become greater", and I asked him: I don't understand you, Lord, and he reminded me that people flattered me, and I recognized by all appearances that the Honor and Glory were to God. But in my heart I liked my name to be mentioned. I

WAS STEALING HIS GLORY! With shame, I asked him for forgiveness and I said, "NEVER LORD LET ME GO TO ANY PLACE IF YOU DON'T GO BEFORE ME. I KNOW NOTHING, I CAN DO NOTHING AND HAVE NOTHING, BUT WITH YOU, GREAT THINGS WILL HAPPEN AND I WILL NEVER STEAL NOT EVEN A PIECE OF YOUR GLORY! NEVER AGAIN".

Then, I said to him: "It would be better, if I had never known you, Lord. You have given to me so much, and I am here rusting. People are sick and with problems, and I am here shut in doors". Until one day my husband told me "I don't want to see you like that, raise up. Tell me what you want to do, I will support you. Just not let the house and children unattended. I know that God will prosper you whatever you embark, and I give you my blessing". I answered to him "I would like to go the neighborhoods and evangelize just as 5 or 6 people are put together to present them (creams or frying pans). I WANT TO PRESENT THEM THE BEST, THE LORD OF THE LORDS AND KING OF THE KINGS".

So I started a new way to evangelize. One friend told me how many women you want together in my house. I will bring 20 together, and we had the first meeting in a neighborhood of my city with excellent results and God's support.

A nice woman that was at FGBMFI went home to see me and told me "you are my leader, wherever you go, I will follow you". We were two serving God now. But the only thing I knew how to do was giving testimony of changed lives, which is the tool we use at the FGBMFI, and in the next meeting, my friend Xochitl gave her testimony. My plan was going to neighborhood and then to another. But God changed the plans because the ladies who were in the first meeting wanted to go to the second one, and I told them let me talk with the one in the following house in turn because I don't know if there is room, as we could be in a "high class" house; the next week we could be in a "very humble" house, and to say the truth, that flourished. The problem my friend and I had is that we didn't know what else to share, they already knew our testimonies. I told her, bring teaching from your church, and I started to buy books in a Christian book shop, and I started to read, I learned and applied part of my life that hadn't been healed regarding the area the book was dealing with. I received the part from God. I remember a topic of a book "How to make you tongue beautiful". It was quite strong, but not to offend, I mentioned myself as an example of murmuring in my life. My friend told me one day, I am surprised about the topics you prepare (as I used a study bible, and prepared more complete topics based on The Bible). She says, "I bring topics that some else prepared, but you prepare them; indeed, God is giving to you more gifts".

I hadn't realized that I was learning something new just for people's needs, and there was always a new testimony in my life, and applied them to the topics I was sharing. Right there I knew how God through so much suffering had prepared me to talk about his marvelous things in different areas of a woman. They identified themselves and received divine healing.

When the group was very prosperous we were going to be 3 years. My husband is given the National Direction of FGBMFI and told me, "I need you to open new groups of ladies" (as the group I left didn't prosper). I cried so much for leaving, and now I was crying because I didn't want to come back and leave the women in the neighborhoods. I had to obey my husband; however, I invited them. Most of them joined the new Group of Ladies, which I represent for about twelve years, and almost twenty years of being happy and active members in the organization.

I THOUGHT THAT HAPPINESS DIDN'T EXIST. I CAME BEING AN UNHAPPY WOMAN, THINKING THAT LIFE WAS LIKE THAT AND THAT ALL MARRIAGES HAD PROBLEMS.

<u>The truth we are not a perfect marriage, but we are ha</u>ppy!

NOW I AM PART OF THE HAPPIEST PEOPLE ON EARTH!

That happiness is at your fingertips.

If your life has been sad and you have lost all hope, we invite you to make the difference in this world in an atmosphere of LOVE, UNITY AND RESPECT.

IF THIS MESSAGE REALLY REACHED YOUR HEART, I INVITE YOU TO MAKE A COMMITMENT.

I recognize that I am not the person that I should be.

I recognize that I don't have what I should have.

I recognize that I have failed along my life.

I repent and decide to make a stop in my life.

Lord Jesus, come into my life and give me a new heart to adore you and I decide to serve you with all what I have.

Even with what I don't have.

AMEN.

This song is to thank God for so much love and changing my life story from SUFFERING TO JOY!

Song

It's you, it's you
The reason for my song
For all what you've given to me
Since I came to this world.

I am grateful to you
As you healed my wounds
You've given joy to me
In the midst of my suffering

What a rare thing!
I didn't know it
When deeper
The pain dives down
More joy there will be in your heart

Pain and sadness are inseparable'
With one you eat
With the other you sleep
Now I understand

How much pain
How much sadness
How much solitude
And I thought
That you hated me
When taking away all what I loved
I felt so abandoned

But you had plans
You were molding me
For something bigger
WHAT A BIG MISTAKE!
I know now no pain
No joy!
Without suffering
I wouldn't reach maturity.

To have your approval
My Jesus
I wished so much to feel loved

I longed for it since a child
I hardened more my heart
And made myself strong based on my pride

You know Lord, I was empty
In this life, resented
At everybody
I wasn't happy

Until you came
And gave me a way out

It's you, it's you
The reason for my song
For everything you've given to me
FOR JOY IN THE MIDST OF
PAIN!

Printed in the United States
By Bookmasters